with their eyes

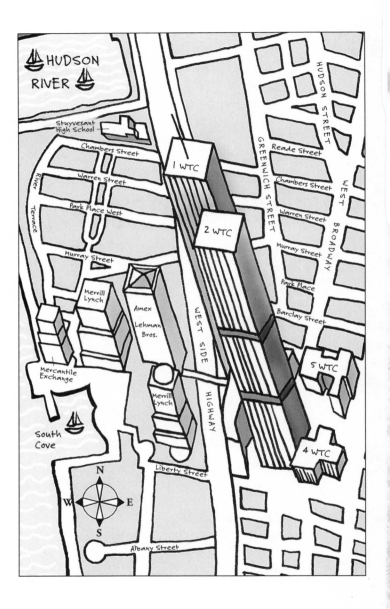

SEPTEMBER 11TH
the view from a high school at ground zero

# with their eyes

edited by
ANNIE THOMS

Created by
Taresh Batra • Anna Belc • Marcel Briones • Catherine Choy • Tim Drinan
Ilena George • Shanleigh Jalea • Lindsay Long-Waldor • Liz O'Callahan
Chantelle Smith • Michael Vogel • Carlos Williams • Christopher M. Yee

photos by ETHAN MOSES

HarperTempest
*An Imprint of HarperCollinsPublishers*

with their eyes

Introduction and chronology copyright © 2002 by Annie Thoms
Text copyright © 2002 by Taresh Batra, Anna Belc, Marcel Briones,
Catherine Choy, Tim Drinan, Ilena George, Shanleigh Jalea,
Lindsay Long-Waldor, Liz O'Callahan, Chantelle Smith, Michael Vogel,
Carlos Williams, Christopher M. Yee, and the New York City
Board of Education
Foreword copyright © 2002 by Anna Deavere Smith
Photographs copyright © 2002 by Ethan Moses

www.harperteen.com

Library of Congress Cataloging-in-Publication Data

With their eyes : September 11th : the view from a high school at ground
zero / edited by Annie Thoms ; created by Taresh Batra . . . [et al.].

p.     cm.

ISBN 0-06-051718-2 (pbk. : alk. paper) — ISBN 0-06-051806-5 (lib.
bdg. : alk. paper)

1. September 11 Terrorist Attacks, 2001—Drama.   2. Stuyvesant High
School (New York, N.Y.)—Drama.   3. High school students—New York
(State)—New York—Drama.   4. High school students' writings, American—
New York (State)—New York.   I. Thoms, Annie.   II. Batra, Taresh.
III. Stuyvesant High School (New York, N.Y.)

PS3600.A1 W47   2002                                        2002004552
812'.04508358—dc21                                                 CIP
                                                                    AC

Typography by Karin Paprocki

First Edition

with their eyes

For the victims of the September 11th attacks,
their families and friends,
and all those who have suffered in the aftermath.

# Contents

## ACT TWO

# Foreword

WITH THEIR EYES, THEIR EARS,
THEIR BODIES, THEIR HEALTHY SKEPTICISM,
AND THEIR HEARTS

When I was told that the students of Stuyvesant High had used a theater-making technique that I developed, to create a play about the events of September 11, 2001, I couldn't have been more flattered. They saw what I could not see. While they were witnessing this history firsthand, I was on a runway at La Guardia Airport, seeing it from afar, as a small puff of smoke. Eventually I, like others around the world, would be dependent on the storytelling of others—the media, or the stories of those who were close enough to see it with their own eyes. Even as I write this, eight months later, many of us are still hearing and learning particulars of that story.

Stuyvesant High School is just four blocks from Ground Zero. Under the direction of an English teacher, Annie Thoms, these students did an original and generous thing in the wake of September 11, 2001. Some went to volunteer for the Red Cross, others took care of their friends, and some tried to give blood. But these students did something more, and something that most of the nation has yet to do, even now, eight months later. They immediately started to create history, and they immediately started to create art.

Recording history and making art might not seem like major strokes on a canvas full of great things that were done—the work of the fire department, the police department, Mayor Giuliani, the President, his cabinet, those who helped neighbors, strangers, those who risked their lives, the journalists who have written stories, the journalists who, for *The New York Times* for example, committed to telling every story of every person who was killed, those who have given money, and others too numerous to mention. What does it mean, then, that these high school students set out to create art, as I say, and to record history on the cusp of a national emergency, an emergency that rocked the nation, and leaves us, even now, quaking?

One of the places I visited in the several days immediately following September 11th was the steps of the Metropolitan Museum of Art. I stopped several people who were entering, and asked what it was they hoped to find in the museum at such a time. One man told me that art has survived war, famine, floods. Art that manages to do so, art that successfully reveals and captures the spirit of its time—the spirit of violence and terror, as well as the spirit of love and celebration—lasts for centuries.

And then what about history? We all know the value of history. Histories are being written about the events of September 11th. Journalism itself is, as we know, history's first draft. The great histories, like the great works of art, will be created after much contemplation, some long after all of us who experienced it are deceased. In fact, the great histories and great works of art will require months, years, decades, centuries of reflection. What's special about this particular history and this particular art?

This particular history is written not just with the eyes, but with the ears and the bodies of these young students. It is critical that they have written this history precisely because it is *their* history, and a history for *their* world and *their* future. We, some of us, who have the authority to speak for many, nonetheless will depend on these teenagers to create the world of the future. How will they bring humanity through its greatest present challenge: the challenge of how to guarantee the survival of the human race through a dramatically fractious time, and a time with enormous technological resources, but very poor human ones?

This history, with all its details, all its particulars, is important. A year from now, ten years from now, the particulars will be erased. It is the erasure of particulars that has, in fact, fostered the kind of coarse segmentation of societies that we have. It is the erasure of particulars that causes us to look at the world in black and white. The very fact that these students were asked to listen for particulars is a first step to making the world a more habitable place.

My generation has created a world where we are rewarded for talk. Look at television any hour of the day and you will see a parade of talk, because talk, you see, is cheaper for television producers to make than fiction. Very little in our society celebrates listening. That these students, with the aid of their teacher and their tape recorders, were required, ultimately, to listen to this talk with all its unfinished sentences, its "uhs," "ums," and "you knows," is already an advance. Could it be that a first step is to create a generation of listeners? You who are reading may be tempted to skip over those "uhs" and "ums" to get to "the point." Know that when you do that, you miss the point. The point is that each individual has a particular story to tell, and the story is more than words: the story is its rhythms and its breaths.

Notice how articulate everyone becomes when we give our attention to much more than "the point." Listen to the words of a freshman, Katie Berringer, as she describes what it was like to go to another school while Stuyvesant was being restored:

*It was kinda like everybody was a freshman.*

And indeed, in those days, all of us New Yorkers, whether we were stuck at airports, required to walk miles home from work, smelling that smell that permeated the air for weeks, or reflecting suddenly on our mortality, both individual and national—everybody was, as this young student says in her own particularly eloquent way, "a freshman."

This book is a blueprint. What these students ultimately did was to make a play in which they played the parts of these individual speakers. They were compelled, then, to empathize with these individuals, to put themselves in another person's words the way, in the past, we have thought metaphorically of putting ourselves in other people's shoes. Could it be that a first step is to create a generation of leaders who can empathize? Could it be that empathy can even serve as a defense against that which could harm us? "Keep your enemies as close as your friends," they used to say. Could it be that we should pour resources into creating laboratories where we learn about human communication with the same seriousness that we study fiber-optic communication?

So, these acting, linguistic historians at Stuyvesant High, a high school perhaps much like any other high school in 2002 where youngsters can stay within their safety zones, dared to wear and learn and *embody* the words of others—fellow students, their teachers, the staff. One of the building staff was in charge of getting things back in order, when he noticed that a particularly important part of the school was missing:

> *But tryin' to get*
> *the building back into sorts . . .*
> *okay*
> *and one of the things that I noticed*
> *on the stage*
> *was the base*
> *of the flag*
> *and no flag.*
> *So I, I was lookin' all over the building for the*
> *flag and I couldn't find it.*

I wondered, when I read that, how many students took note of that flag before September 11th. I'm sure they do now. Even in a time of devotion to our country, these students found a key part of what makes America great. What is key to our greatness is that we always find time, room, space, venue, for critique. What is key to our greatness is a diversity of ideas and the spirit of debate.

A senior, Max Willens, spoke with great passion, and in

a very articulate way, about something that has been permeating our culture for the last decade—and that is our tendency to make a circus out of that which is in front of us, to make a spectacle. And yet, the benefit of this critique, and the benefit of having it in a play, is that it can be cause for discussion. A live performance gives us what television news never will. It gives us the opportunity, in the flesh, to respond. We can also break the conventions of some audiences. The job of an audience can be not just to applaud and say congratulations, but to have real dialogue. This young man's opinion of those who came to pay respects, if enacted by an actor elsewhere, would be, and it should be, a great point of discussion and disagreement. As such, it would create a special kind of community around its recitation—a thinking, analytical community.

> *There were people there* all the time,
> *and they weren't even New Yorkers,*
> *they weren't even people visiting some, you know,*
> *taking a look at something that used to* be *there,*
> *something that they used to know.*
> *They were people from Kansas and Oklahoma,*
> *    and, you know,*
> *Missouri, who had seen those places on postcards.*

*And they wanted to buy hats and pins,*
*and wanted to sing "God Bless America" and*
*   things like that.*
*Which made me sick.*

*The pictures,*
*the pictures were probably what really did it*
*   for me.*
*There were these disposable cameras,*
*the kind that people, you know,*
*whip out for trips to Disneyland or the*
*   Grand Canyon, you know,*
*those yellow plastic things, you know,*
*where everyone crowds around and the flashes*
*   make those little annoying*
*yellow sounds.*
*And I had to, I dunno . . .*
*one time, someone actually asked me to take a*
*   photograph of them,*
*of them looking,*
*kind of standing in a solemn pose with the*
*   wreckage as a backdrop,*
*and I couldn't do it.*
*I nearly threw the camera at them, I just . . .*
*I couldn't . . .*
*it made me sick.*

A play is not alive until human breath takes on the words. I hope that people around the country, and indeed around the world, whether fifth graders, twelfth graders, college students, adult community theater groups, church groups, or PTAs, produce this play, and say the words of those from Stuyvesant High who saw with their eyes and heard with their ears, in their particular way.

We have here one of the very ironies of history. Eventually, those particulars, which are so critical in the moment, so critical to our individuality, wash out over time. Centuries from now, hard as it is to believe, some high school in a foreign land will struggle to play a play like this one, wondering what in the world an expression like "like" means, or, for that matter, "dunno." Centuries from now, even our enemies, those who currently threaten our existence, might play such a play. And centuries from now, we might play such a play with their history.

This is what has happened, over time. The Greeks, the Romans, the Africans, the Asians—all over the world, the plays of wars and famines, and victories, the plays of sad dark days, and the plays of better years, better celebrations, have been played, have outlasted the very disputes that inspired them. I say to all of you young students, who might speak these words out of your own attempt to understand what it must have felt like to be so near this tragic, terrifying, heartrending moment: Be strong. Be new. Be you.

ANNA DEAVERE SMITH
*Actress, Playwright, Professor*
Director of the Institute on the Arts and Civic Dialogue
New York University
April 28, 2002

ANNA DEAVERE SMITH is an actor, director, playwright, and teacher whose work combines the journalistic technique of interviewing her subjects with the art of interpreting their words through performance. The MacArthur Foundation awarded Ms. Smith a prestigious fellowship in 1996, saying she "has created a new form of theater—a blend of theatrical art, social commentary, journalism and intimate reverie." Her plays, *Fires in the Mirror: Crown Heights, Brooklyn and Other Identities*; *Twilight: Los Angeles 1992*; and *House Arrest*, have been performed across the country. Smith has won many awards for her work in the theater, including two Obies and two Tony nominations. She is the founding director of the Institute on the Arts and Civic Dialogue, dedicated to creating art for social change. Her book, *Talk to Me*, was published by Random House in 2000, and explores the roles of the press and the American presidency in our society. Ms. Smith is a tenured professor at New York University, with an appointment to Tisch School of the Arts and an affiliation with the NYU School of Law. She was recently appointed Artist-in-Residence at MTV Networks. A native of Baltimore, she currently lives in New York City.

# Acknowledgments

To all the interviewees, for their extraordinary words, and for allowing themselves to be portrayed on stage and in print.

To Anna Deavere Smith, for her inspirational work.

To the Stuyvesant administration for their support: Principal Stanley Teitel, Assistant Principal of Student Services Eugene Blaufarb, and Assistant Principal of Organization Steven Satin.

For invaluable mentorship and insight: Dr. Steven Shapiro, Assistant Principal, English Department.

To Kerneth Levigion, Richard Realmuto, and Renée Levine for going above and beyond the call of duty, every day.

For financial support: the Stuyvesant High School Alumni Association, especially Cindy Nieves, for her help with all the forms.

To my colleagues in the English Department, especially Holly Ojalvo for her great friendship and editing skills, Amy Katz for being a fabulous Coordinator of Student Affairs, Eric Grossman for his support as Acting Chairman this spring, and Tim Simonds for beginning the tradition of the Winter Drama several years ago.

To the staff of *The Spectator* for their hard work and high standards, especially Abigail Deutsch for her article "An Administration in Crisis" and her interview with Chancellor Levy.

To the unsung heroes of Stuyvesant: the custodial staff, the dining hall staff, and the school safety officers.

For help at the inception of *with their eyes*, the Stuyvesant Theater Community Slate: Anna Gressel, Lindsey Gurin, Sarah Kaufmann, Alex Pearlman, and Hallie Saltz.

For help with the logistics of the show: Jessica Schumer, for running ticket sales and handling the money; Kristen Aufiero, for last-minute program-stapling; and the ushers from Arista for their professionalism.

For lots and lots of copying: Elhadji Diop in the Stuyvesant copy room.

To Ethan Moses, for his beautiful photographs.

To Ann Moore, for being our fairy godmother on a plane to Palm Springs.

To Ann Frkovich, for introducing me to the work of Anna Deavere Smith during our time at Teachers College.

To Judith Kocela Hawk, for making me want to become a teacher.

To my family, for sparking a love of reading and writing, and supporting me in everything I've ever done.

To the families of the cast and crew, for their patience and support, and for producing such extraordinary kids.

To Tui Sutherland, for bringing this project to HarperCollins and shepherding it through the necessary stages with warmth, excitement, and intelligence.

To my husband, Jeff Bolas, for living every minute of this with me and for being my best editor as well as my best friend.

And finally, to Ilena, Lindsay, Michael, Taresh, Anna, Marcel, Cathy, Tim, Shanleigh, Liz, Chantelle, Carlos, and Chris, without whose talent, heart, and energy these stories could not have been told.

**THE DIRECTORS, PRODUCERS, AND CAST OF *WITH THEIR EYES*:**

*front row, l to r:* Chantelle Smith, Catherine Choy, Lindsay Long-Waldor, Anna Belc, Taresh Batra, Shanleigh Jalea

*back row, l to r:* Michael Vogel, Carlos Williams, Marcel Briones, Liz O'Callahan, Tim Drinan, Christopher M. Yee, Annie Thoms, Ilena George

# Introduction

I teach high school English four blocks from ground zero. On the morning of September 11th, I walked up the subway stairs and onto Chambers Street, as I do every morning on my way to work. The sky was a bright blue, the day crisp, but as I left the subway station I saw huge clouds of gray smoke hanging in the air above me. The street was filled with people, everybody staring up. So I looked too.

The World Trade Center was on fire, flames leaping from an angry gash in the side of the north tower. I asked the man standing next to me what had happened, and he told me about the planes. The second one, he said, had hit ten minutes earlier. We stood there for a moment, watching papers swirl from the windows of the towers, watching small black objects fall. Then I realized that the small black objects were people. I caught my breath and turned down the hill, toward school.

Stuyvesant High School is four blocks north of the World Trade Center, at the western edge of Manhattan. From its windows, students, faculty, and staff have clear views of the Hudson River, the Statue of Liberty, and, from the south side, the World Trade Center. On September 11th, this meant that hundreds of Stuyvesant students saw the planes hit, saw people jumping from their office windows, saw the towers fall. In less than two hours after the first plane hit the north tower, the school was evacuated—over 3,200 students, faculty, and staff moving safely up the West Side Highway. On that day, and in the weeks that followed, our building became a triage center and base of operations for the rescue and recovery effort. We were out of school for ten days, and then relocated for two weeks to a high school in Brooklyn before resuming classes in our building in October.

Stuyvesant is a magnet school, drawing high-achieving students from all five boroughs of New York City. This makes for a diverse student body, but it also made it difficult, after September 11th, for students and faculty to meet as a community—public transportation was disrupted, and our one common neighborhood had been taken away. September 11th was the fifth day of classes of a new year; we had barely learned each other's names, and suddenly we were all separated.

As a teacher, one of the hardest things about the first days after the attacks was being completely cut off from my students. I felt helpless, unable to talk to them, unable to use my classroom as a place to share our experience and process some of what had happened to us. At home, I wrote. I contacted relatives and friends, I watched TV, I cried. One of my colleagues, from her home in Brooklyn, alerted me to a couple of student-run websites where Stuyvesant students were talking to each other, posting hundreds of messages about their own experiences on the day of the attacks, and their reactions since then. Reading their accounts, I was struck by the number of different stories they told, and the strength of their need to tell those stories. An idea began to form.

Late last year, I had become the faculty adviser for the Stuyvesant Theater Community. In that position, I knew I would be responsible for this year's Winter Drama. What if, I thought, we created a play in which Stuyvesant students were able to tell their own stories, and the stories of others in our community, about our experiences on September 11th?

I looked to the work of playwright and actress Anna Deavere Smith, especially her plays *Fires in the Mirror*, which focuses on the aftermath of the 1991 Crown Heights riots, and *Twilight: Los Angeles*, which explores the issues surrounding the L.A. riots of 1992. For each of these plays, Smith interviewed hundreds of people on tape, creating monologues from their spoken words. She then performed in the character and voice of the people she had interviewed, producing in each one-woman show a vivid, complex picture of a community's reaction to violent tragedy.

This format, with a larger cast, seemed ideal for our situation. I broached the idea to the Stuyvesant Theater Community Slate, and together we decided to try it out. In late November, we chose a student director, Ilena George, and two student producers, Lindsay Long-Waldor and Michael Vogel.

Ilena, Lindsay, Michael and I set out to assemble a cast which would represent the diversity of our school— Stuyvesant is over 50 percent Asian and just over 40 percent white, with the remaining number made up of black and Latino students. Many of our students are immigrants or first-generation Americans. We visited a number of Stuyvesant's cultural clubs, and put out the word that we were looking for cast members from all four grades. Of the forty-five or so students who auditioned, reading monologues from *Fires in the Mirror*, we chose ten.

They were three seniors: Marcel Briones, Liz O'Callahan, and Chantelle Smith; two juniors: Anna Belc and Shanleigh Jalea; three sophomores: Catherine Choy, Tim Drinan, and Christopher Yee; and two freshmen: Taresh Batra and Carlos Williams. They were five boys and five girls; they were white, black, Asian, and Middle Eastern; they were immigrants and kids born in New York City. Few of them had acted at Stuyvesant before; in a school of over three thousand students, few knew each other at all.

At our first meeting, the atmosphere in the room was a little strained. We did ice-breaking introductions, and then moved into our first brainstorming session: Who should the actors interview? We came up with a list of specific names and of general categories: Liz wanted to interview "a freshman nobody knows"; several of us wanted the perspective of a Muslim student; actors called out names of friends they thought would give great interviews. Ilena read the completed list aloud, and the cast wrote down their top choices, including students, faculty, and building staff.

Each cast member then set out with a small tape recorder to interview two or three people. Following Anna Deavere Smith's example, we did not limit the actors to playing only characters of their own race or gender. The people each actor interviewed were the people he or she played, regardless of their physical dissimilarity. Each interviewee was offered the option of remaining anonymous; several did.

It was important to all of us that the play not be focused exclusively on the events of September 11th, but also address the days, weeks, and months afterward. Because we wanted to elicit stories about a variety of subjects, the actors did not ask all their interviewees the same questions, though there were some common ones: Where were you on September 11th, and what did you see? Have we gotten back to normal?

What's "normal" to you? What do you think we need to talk about?

The actors recorded their interviews, then began the painful process of transcribing them word for word, including all the *um*s, *like*s, and *you know*s of normal speech. They edited these transcripts into poem-monologues, including line breaks to suggest pauses in the interviewees' speech patterns. The goal in creating these monologues was not to whittle down each interviewee's words to get at a few major points. It was to capture the ways individual people express themselves in speech, sometimes stumbling, sometimes dancing around and toward a subject for several minutes before finding what they feel are the right words. A few interviews did not yield enough material for a monologue, but extraordinarily, most did—people had so much to say, and were so eloquent in saying it, that it was just a matter of editing and shaping their words.

Our first rehearsal with the completed monologues took place in the theater in mid-December. We sat in a circle on the stage, and for over two hours the cast members read aloud. Ilena and I had seen many of the monologues before as we worked with the actors on editing, but this was the first time any of us had heard them all together. We listened, hearing already the work that each actor had done in beginning to take on the voice of his or her characters. I jotted down ideas for the titles of each monologue, and several cast members wrote down ideas for the title of the play.

The listening was intense. In interviewing, and in editing, each story had been alone, singular. Now, we heard the stories speak to each other, painting a picture of anger and panic, of hope and strength, of humor and resilience. During and after each new monologue, we teared up, laughed, wiped our eyes. For each of us, there were lines in one or two monologues that sounded utterly familiar—things we had said, or thought, ourselves. For each of us, there were details and reactions we had never thought of before. When the last monologue had finished, we sat and looked at each other, amazed.

Over the next hour, we talked about titles, deciding on *with their eyes* as the best title for the play. Then we went for pizza, and, crowded into three tables in the back of the restaurant, determined the order of the monologues. We didn't want to put them in chronological order, but rather to shape them into a coherent emotional whole, with highs and lows, themes, resonances. We stayed until after nine-thirty, completing a six-hour rehearsal, and drifted away to our separate subway stops calling out each other's names.

That was the night that set the tone for the rest of our rehearsals—focused, yes, but also warm, open, and riotously funny. By the end of the night we had in-jokes, and Lindsay had begun keeping a notebook to write down the hysterical things everybody said. The split in the ages of our cast members worked to make them sweetly protective of each other, and the jokes just kept coming throughout the rest of our rehearsals. In many ways, I think that we could not have created *with their eyes* without this atmosphere. Working with such heavy material, we needed lightness among ourselves.

In rehearsal, as in creating the monologues, there was a lot of individual work before we brought the show together as a whole. Each actor listened to his or her audiotapes over and over, capturing the rhythms and vocal patterns of each interviewee, and practicing the interviewee's stance and mannerisms. We were aware from the outset of the fine line between portrayal and caricature, especially in the case of "You Need Hope," for which Marcel had interviewed two students from P.S. 721, the special education school within Stuyvesant. Marcel spoke with the families of the students, and researched ways to portray them accurately and without offending anyone. Other actors did field work to prepare themselves for performance: Shanleigh skipped lunch to sit in on Matt Polazzo's social studies class several days in a row, taking notes on his walk. For every actor in the show, the prospect of having their interviewees come to see themselves played on stage was a little daunting.

In the few weeks before the show, as the set took shape,

Ilena took on the task of blocking the actors. She created a computer-drawn layout of the set pieces and penciled in diagrams for each section, blocking silent scenes among the nine actors behind the one who, at a given moment, was delivering his or her monologue. All ten actors remained on-stage at all times, changing costume in front of the audience. In the staging, as in the monologues themselves, we tried to avoid being cheesy or maudlin, to avoid tear-jerking moments or empty displays of patriotism and unity. We felt there was unity inherent in these stories, the natural unity of a disparate community.

Despite our focus on bringing out stories which had not yet been heard, many members of the Stuyvesant community were opposed to the idea of a play about September 11th. They felt that there had been enough talk about the day, enough talk about our reactions—they wanted to move on. Some of them came to the play; some did not. We performed *with their eyes* on February 8 and 9, 2002, to an audience which included friends from outside Stuyvesant and members of several media organizations. Both shows were received with standing ovations.

I've been asked many times over the past six months how the Stuyvesant community is doing, how we have recovered.

There is no easy answer. We are more than 3,200 students, teachers, and building staff—there are as many reactions as there are people in the building. Each of us knows our own story: where we were on September 11th, what we thought, how it has changed us. Each of us knows the stories of our friends. But even within a single building, there are thousands of stories waiting to be heard. Here are twenty-three of them. Listen.

ANNIE THOMS
March 2002

# Chronology of Events

8:48 A.M.—The first plane hits the north tower. Many at Stuyvesant hear the bang, and feel the school tremble.

8:50–9:02 A.M.—Principal Stanley Teitel contacts the school superintendent's office, and determines it is safest to keep all students inside the building. Over the loudspeaker, an administration official informs the Stuyvesant community that a "small plane" has hit the World Trade Center.

9:03 A.M.—The second plane hits the south tower. Many students, faculty, and staff see the collision, and watch the ensuing fire from the building's south-facing windows. Some turn on the televisions which hang in each Stuyvesant classroom. Phone communications from the building are jammed.

9:04–9:49 A.M.—FBI and Secret Service agents enter the building, and begin to set up Stuyvesant as a command post and triage center. Teitel asks the agent in charge, "What are the chances of those towers coming down?" The agent responds,

"No chance." Teitel announces over the loudspeaker that all students are to stay in the building. At the bell at 9:25, students move to their next class.

9:50 A.M.—The south tower collapses. Stuyvesant shakes. Lights flicker, and television pictures turn to static—the television antenna on top of the World Trade Center is gone.

9:51–10:29 A.M.—Assistant Principal of Student Services Eugene Blaufarb announces over the loudspeaker that students should report to their homerooms. After a brief administrative meeting, he announces that Stuyvesant students and faculty are to evacuate the building, exiting through two doors on the north, sheltered side only. Students are joined on their walk uptown by pedestrians fleeing lower Manhattan, many covered head-to-toe with thick white dust.

The teachers and paraprofessionals working at P.S. 721, the special education school housed in rooms on the top three floors of Stuyvesant, begin to evacuate their students from the school. Most of them are wheelchair-bound. They take the freight elevators down to the first floor and begin their journey to a safe school uptown.

10:30 A.M.—The north tower collapses, sending a wave of dust up from the World Trade Center and over Stuyvesant. The evacuation continues, as over 3,200 members of the Stuyvesant community funnel through the two doors.

10:31 A.M. and later—Stuyvesant's theater and gyms continue to be used as a command center. All students and faculty have safely vacated the building. Many staff members, including school safety officers and custodians, remain to help the rescue workers and keep the building running.

Public transportation has been suspended. Students and faculty walk uptown in small groups, splitting off from each other to go to their homes or the homes of friends nearby.

WEDNESDAY, SEPTEMBER 12

All New York City schools are closed.

THURSDAY, SEPTEMBER 13–
WEDNESDAY, SEPTEMBER 19

As other New York City schools reopen, Stuyvesant and several other schools in the area remain closed. Stuyvesant's building continues to be used as a command center and staging area for the World Trade Center rescue effort. Thousands of tons of supplies are stored there, and rescue workers are fed, clothed, and housed. Classrooms are filled with clothing and food; cots line the hallways. Many members of the Stuyvesant staff work round-the-clock shifts to aid the rescue workers.

Stuyvesant students, living all over the five boroughs of New York, communicate with each other by e-mail. On internet message boards, they tell each other their stories and share information.

On September 16th, the first Sunday after the attacks, over four hundred Stuyvesant students gather in Greenwich Village to paint two eighty-foot murals: a tree of life growing out of rubble, and a banner honoring New York's heroes.

Stuyvesant's administration and Parents' Association negotiate with the Board of Education, trying to find an alternate site at which to reopen Stuyvesant. Martin Luther King, Jr. High School, in uptown Manhattan, is proposed as a possibility, but ultimately Brooklyn Technical High School is chosen.

## THURSDAY, SEPTEMBER 20

Stuyvesant reopens on a split schedule at Brooklyn Technical High School. At the opening-day assembly in Brooklyn Tech's auditorium, four times larger than the theater at Stuyvesant, there is 98% student attendance. The Stuyvesant community listens to speeches by Principal Stanley Teitel, Student Union (SU) President Jukay Hsu, and officials from the Board of Education.

## FRIDAY, SEPTEMBER 21–
## FRIDAY, OCTOBER 5

Stuyvesant and Brooklyn Tech share one building. Brooklyn Tech's 4,000 students attend class from 7:30 A.M. to 1:15 P.M. Stuyvesant's 3,030 students attend class from 1:30 P.M. to 6:30 P.M., in twenty-six-minute periods.

Stuyvesant and Brooklyn Tech are academic rivals, and a certain amount of tension exists between the two student populations. Stuyvesant students are at a disadvantage in the sprawling floor plan of Brooklyn Tech, where rooms are referred to by floor, compass direction, and room number (1E22, 3W44). Many Stuy students find themselves bewildered by separate up and down staircases.

In English classes, Stuyvesant students answer thousands of letters written by students in schools across the country and as far away as Japan.

On October 2, *The Spectator*, Stuyvesant's school newspaper, put out a special full-color, magazine-style issue focusing on the events of September 11th. The student-written articles and student photos receive praise and media attention across the city. In November, the issue is reprinted as an insert in *The New York Times*.

Negotiations over the date of the reopening of Stuyvesant's building continue. Officials in charge of the rescue operation at ground zero leave the building, which is professionally cleaned to remove the dust from the towers' collapse and the rescue effort.

TUESDAY, OCTOBER 9

Stuyvesant reopens in its own building, and classes resume on a normal schedule. The return of students and faculty is covered by several major media organizations, and attended by Senator Charles Schumer, United Federation of Teachers President Randi Weingarten and Schools Chancellor Harold

O. Levy. Levy declares the building safe, and pledges to work from offices in Stuyvesant for the next several days, saying, "If the whole thing weren't safe, I wouldn't be here."

The area below Chambers Street remains closed to pedestrians. Access to Stuyvesant is tightly controlled by the New York City Police Department. Recovery efforts are visible from the south-facing windows of the building. The other area schools, including two smaller high schools, one junior high school, and two elementary schools, remain in their alternate locations.

## OCTOBER–NOVEMBER

Extra security precautions are taken within Stuyvesant, and more school safety officers are assigned to the school. Students are required to wear their ID cards around their necks. For the remainder of the fall semester, they are not allowed to go out of the building for lunch. Visits by recent alumni over Thanksgiving are prohibited. There is some grumbling about these measures from the student body, but general compliance.

On October 12, Chancellor Levy leaves Stuyvesant to move back to his own offices at Board of Education headquarters in Brooklyn.

The air quality in and around Stuyvesant is heavily monitored by inspectors hired by the Board of Education and the Stuyvesant Parents' Association. Air testing equipment is set up in school hallways, and carried from room to room by air-quality testers. The results of these tests are interpreted by a number of experts, and there is disagreement about whether the air is completely safe.

Several students come to school dressed as air-quality testers for Halloween.

On a pier just north of Stuyvesant, the city government sets up barges which are used to sort debris from the World Trade Center. These barges become the focus of concern and protest by the Parents' Association, and by members of the faculty and staff, worried about their contribution to poor air quality.

On November 12, American Airlines Flight 587 crashes into a residential neighborhood in Rockaway, Queens. All 260 passengers and five Rockaway residents on the ground are killed. National airports are closed as government agencies investigate the possibility that the crash is another terrorist attack. Shortly, however, it is determined to have been an accident.

Stuyvesant continues to receive both media attention and gifts from around the world, including three thousand small potted plants intended to help combat heightened levels of carbon dioxide. In mid-November, AOL Time Warner donates individual duffel bags filled with gifts to the faculty and staff of each school in the ground zero area.

The cast of *with their eyes* is chosen, and begins to interview students, faculty, and staff around the school, in preparation for their performance on February 8 and 9, 2002.

# Act One

## OVERTURE

### Kevin Zhang, sophomore

I saw this
*huge* plane it was . . .
it looked much bigger than the first one,
it just,
it looked like one of those jets, you know, in the movies,
you know, Air Force One or something,
   one of those big jets.
It was one of those and it just hits—
it hit the building right there.


### Katherine Fletcher, English teacher

I noticed it enough to say to my class
what was that
sort of casually

I wasn't scared or alarmed I just sort of said what
what was that
and someone said
thunder
and I was like no
it's not thunder
it must have been a truck
it was like a sound of a truck like hitting something
    on a street or
you know how sometimes you'll hear something like that.


Hudson Williams-Eynon, freshman

We all went to Art.
My art class is on the tenth floor
turned
facing north so
we couldn't see anything but
everyone was looking out
the windows
so
the teacher was like
"You know,

this might sound stupid and everything
but I still want you guys to draw.
You can tell your kids that when
the World Trade Center was
y'know
attacked
you guys were drawing
contour drawings."


## Juan Carlos Lopez, School Safety Agent

I got this weird transmission
the strangest transmission in my life
that a plane hit the World Trade Center
and I ran into that computer room to see.
I haven't gotten back into that office.
The recollection of what I saw is framed in that window,
like if I had to draw you a picture I would
have to draw the window frame as well.
I'm a little apprehensive,
just looking at these banners I get a little choked up.
So I—I fear going into that office
I might lose my composure.

But, it's been long enough that maybe I could go into that
    office
and take it in
but I, I—
you know in a way I don't feel ready, I don't.


## Renée Levine, Building Coordinator

I was in Mr. Satin's office
on the second floor.
I went to the window
and I looked down—not out
not up
I looked down.
I saw people running across the courtyard of . . .
of I.S. 89.
I thought a truck had crashed
into the playground.
I heard someone yell outside
and then I went onto the bridge
and I saw
I saw
the . . .

gash in the side of the building
the flames coming out
I went back inside
and I put on the TV
and they were saying that it was a small commuter plane
   that had crashed
into the building.
The first reaction was *ohh it's not terrorism.*
Then the second one hit
and I knew.


Katie Berringer, freshman


We didn't know what was going on
so when we see this like
psychopathic lady running down the hallway
like "I need to call my mother, I need to call my mother!"
and we're like
*What is wrong with HER?*
and we didn't know what was going on so we were like
laughing at her.
But then we heard that thing on the speakers
but we still thought it was like

tiny and they were telling us out of respect
like when that guy died and everyone had a moment
   of silence.
We thought it was something like that—
but I saw my friend and he was telling me
like about all these things he was seeing out the windows
and I was like *holy shit*
this is big.


Jennifer Suri,
Assistant Principal, Social Studies


There were students who came into my office to use
   the phone
to touch base with their parents
to see if they were okay . . .
and there were actually many of them crowded into my room
and the electricity went out
momentarily and the lights started flickering
   and everyone screamed
and dropped to the floor, frightened.
And I just tried to comfort them.

## Tony Qian, sophomore

Once we came out we saw the big smoke . . .
I dunno,
when people started talking about this was a . . .
terrorist attack
I was completely,
uh,
I just couldn't accept that.
I dunno.
I was just coming into myself that
this wasn't the case, that
this was probably just an accident.
Yeah, well, when people say that, um,
when you're . . .
sometimes your rationality fails you during a time of crisis.
I never believed that until that day.
I just couldn't think correctly.
So, what can I say?
But,
but, uh,
the soot and the dust was so dense we couldn't see anything.
So,
I didn't know that both were,
you know,
down, already.

## Anonymous male custodian

When it happened
I watched the buildings fall,
I was in my house.
My wife was on the phone.
She woke me up.
I work nights.
I was sleeping when it was happening.
She woke me up and told me to turn on the TV.
And ya know
I saw the planes hit
ahh . . .
like unbelievable
ya know what I mean.
It was like . . .
I was just sayin' *it must be a dream, it must be a dream.*


## Matt Polazzo, Social Studies teacher

Well, I biked into school that morning
uh, but
it didn't happen while I was on my bike, I was in the, um
the Social Studies office in room 302 and

I was

fiddling around on the computer and

I don't think I heard the first impact

and if I did, I didn't realize it

but I walked out into the

hallway, and I

noticed immediately that all the kids were looking strange

  in this room

and I think it was Ms. Kelly's room

in room 304.

They were all

clustered up against the windows and

you know that's the en—

that's the big symbol that something's going down—

if you see someone else looking.

Roman,

one of my

homeroom kids, was running out.

He said something like

"Oh shit, Polazzo, they

blew up the World Trade Center again!"

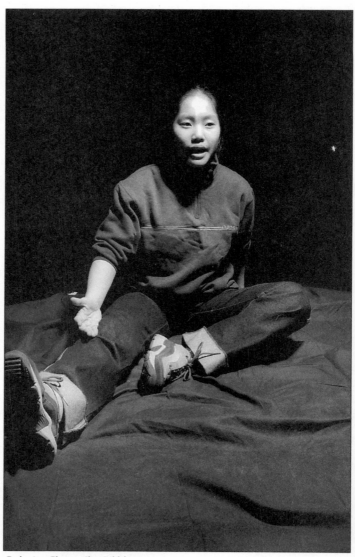

Catherine Choy as Ilya Feldsherov

# PIECE OF MY HOME

## Ilya Feldsherov, senior

*Ilya is eighteen years old, an immigrant from the Ukraine.*
*He is captain of the gymnastics team, lean and very muscular.*
*He has a badly injured right knee, which pains him*
*and makes his walk stiff-legged. He rubs his knee as he speaks,*
*getting up from his chair after a while to sit on the floor*
*and stretch out his leg. He wears tight jeans, worn sneakers,*
*a tight muscle shirt, and a fleece jacket. He speaks matter-of-*
*factly, with a slight Ukrainian accent.*

Well, September 11th was also my senior picture day.
So I get up in the morning
and I took half an hour
fixing my hair.
Put on a suit, really uncomfortable dress shoes,
big shirt, and I didn't want to carry all my books around
so I thought I'd just leave everything in my locker.
Well, yeah, I just
recently got my cell phone,
so I was carrying that around the whole day.

So I get up in the morning.

Came to school normal,

came to school early . . .

put all my stuff in my locker

and I was only carrying a folder around.

I was in French class

when it happened . . .

I swear I didn't hear anything, but my French teacher

my French teacher

that I swear is like a hundred and sixty-five years old

she comes in about twenty minutes late.

Well, she needs to scan our books we need for the year.

And she starts, "Well, I was looking in the office for

a scanner and the

chairperson says

well, a plane hit the World Trade Center,"

and she says, "Well, okay

I still need the scanner"

and he says, "No no no don't you know what I said

a plane hit the World Trade Center."

"Well, okay, I still need the scanner."

So yeah, she gets the scanner. And she comes into class and

she tells us this.

And we all . . . we all

laugh,

cuz we don't know what's going on.

So we're . . . okay . . .

the plane hit . . .

the plane hit . . . I—

it didn't really register, you know.

We heard it from her . . . and okay

she goes on scanning our books.

So then I walk into physics

which is right after French.

That's when I see the building, and then I see the smoke.

And I'm like *Holy Shit!*

that's not, uh, you know

that's NOT just her being delusional.

Something pretty bad's going on.

And then I felt it.


We sat there in physics watching for a while.

And one of my friends was going crazy

because his parents were boarding a plane that morning
     to go somewhere

and they got on the plane at like 7:50 and he was going
     crazy,

he wasn't sure what plane it was or where it came from.

He was really worried about them

and I was telling him there's really no chance of them being

on that plane cuz of all

whatever factors.

Probably going another direction.

And we just sat there for a while.

And we all stared out the window and

we are all just numbed

and we saw people running.

And then about twenty minutes into the period

the top of the building fell.

And then we—

we were watching the building fall,

we're watching it from a distance.

I usually don't get afraid easily but

I became

I was really afraid.

I was—I just felt it, *this is really happening!*

*This just happens in*

*bad movies.*

*This isn't happening, this isn't real life,*

and I just got scared.

And one of my friends

that sat next to me in physics,

her mom works in the World Trade Center.
And she was really worried.
And I went down to the . . .
second floor
to try my cell phone,
to see if it was working
so I could call,
so I could call wherever she wanted to call,
wherever her mom was,
to see if she was okay.
But, the phones weren't working then
and so . . .
I left my cell phone in the locker,
with my book bag and everything else.
Funny thing—
I had a sandwich that morning
which was also in my book bag
which I-I—
left in the school for the next,
however many weeks we weren't in school.
And it was kinda funky when we got back!

So we came back up and we sat through physics
and so, uh, half the building falls . . .

half the period ended.
And we went to homeroom and
I saw my friend, one of my best friends, Julia,
she's one of my best friends from freshman year
and she was—she was just shaking.
And I just held her.
And we were all like not saying anything,
we were all just standing there,
thinking like *oh my god!*
and
some people were hysterical.
We started evacuating
and then we saw people crying in the staircases.
And I had another friend whose
uncle worked in the World Trade Center.
And again I went downstairs to see if my cell phone was
    working . . .
she was really worried and crying
everywhere you looked it's like someone had a mother
a father
and it was, you know
it just felt really close to home. And it was like, you know,
scary that you realize you almost lose your mortality.
It's right there.

What if?
What if it was closer?

I left my cell phone at school
and I wish I'd had my cell phone . . .
and I remember walking uptown
in my suit and my shoes,
and feeling *really* uncomfortable
and wishing I had
brought sneakers or shoes to change into
or thinking maybe I should stop by a store
and, uh, buy slippers
and
just carry my shoes.
After we left the school
I chilled with my friends.
We ate, we talked, we wasted a lot of time . . . we hung out.

Oh, my dad—
my dad he just sorta nodded when I first came in . . .
and we sat down at dinner
and he poured himself vodka and he poured me some
    cognac . . .
and then, you know, I had

two shots and I just went straight to bed.
My dad didn't really say anything.
He just sort of
had a look like
*I know I could tell you went through a lot*
*and I'm not gonna bother you with all these questions.*

I mean, it feels weird being the center of
a school's project.
I mean—
yeah, that's great,
but we . . .
we really are fine.
Okay,
GOD BLESS US
but
we really are fine.

The first day when I came back
and when I walked past
everything was still smoking,
the ruins sticking out of the ground and
I was like DAMN and couldn't have much of . . .
I mean, I had a reaction.

I just felt some piece of New York was,
I mean, it's been home to me most of my life,
twelve years . . .
It was a piece of my home
well, one of my homes . . .
well, the best home,
it was like, GOD . . .
a little bit of everything.

Tim Drinan as Max Willens

# BAG MAN

## Max Willens, senior

*Max is a tall, red-haired eighteen-year-old with round glasses and a ring on his left pinky. He wears a hooded sweatshirt and three layers of pants: boxers, gym shorts, and baggy pants, the tops of which are all visible when he lifts his arms. He folds the cuffs of his sweatshirt inward upon themselves and rubs his ring with his left thumb throughout. He has a deep voice and speaks with an emphasis on the beginnings of his words, which often makes him sound angrier than he actually is. He usually places his weight on one foot at a time.*

Well, I dunno. I guess my story is different from everyone else's.

For a while I didn't have a house. I was . . . I was living in different places.

I had a bag of clothes.

I had a, *one*, plastic bag that sometimes got filled with stuff if we went to

like Kmart to get underwear or socks.

Sometimes a T-shirt or two.
But I had a bag that was what I carried with me—
I had my backpack, next to a plastic bag, and that was,
that was who I was for a while.

And then I went to live with my cousin upstate for a while
    which was . . .
pretty weird.
I, I was—basically all I did up there was sit, and
we, um, we were out on this lake—
Great Sacandaga Lake, it's called—
just sitting and, I just, I would sit there and just stare at it,
    you know?
When I wasn't staring at that I was, you know,
shooting,
shooting hoops on a tired old, you know,
backboard that they put up on over the drive,
over the driveway,
Sometimes reading, sometimes sleeping.

For a while it was nice to sleep a lot because
you know, you don't have to think as much.
If you have to read,
you read,

you think.

You sleep a lot and you don't have to deal with it.

I don't dream for some reason, I never have.

Not much, anyway.

And I didn't dream during this either.

No nightmares, no nothing,

I just slept. *[Pause]*

Kinda like,

kinda like Jack Burton in *All the King's Men,*

just the great sleep.

I just sat there or just stayed in bed as long as I could.

Then I'd wake up, and you know, do anything to occupy
    the time. It was,

I dunno . . .

I was the Bag Man for another couple of days, you know?


Then we finally got to, I finally got to go back to my house
    to get some

stuff,

and that was,

that was really

something.

We, um, we took the train down,

I think it was the 6,

and we got out,

and just, the air, was the first thing.

I'm sure everyone else has talked about the air,

but it was probably something that, like,

my *body* is not going to forget.

It's just that, it's interesting, it was like,

the, the air felt on the outside like something that you
    might smell at a,

or feel at a barbecue,

but it didn't, it . . . it hurt you.

It hurt your windpipe.

I could feel like, things collecting on my esophagus or
    on my lungs,

and I don't think that is something that I will ever forget.


So then we finally get home, and it was—

my house looked like a black-and-white photograph.

We'd left the windows open that day.

Everything was gray or black, or even just a, a dusted color.

Everything was just—I felt like I was, you know, walking
    into a portrait,

The house just . . .

it was just dirty.

When things are dirty there's—it's like a multi-sensory thing, it was like,

I guess I'm saying it again,

it was walking into a photograph.

It was just dirty. . . . It wasn't even my house anymore.


But my room . . . which . . .

I dunno why . . .

it was clean. Things looked fine.

Everything was the same color it was when I remembered it.

My carpet. My blue comforter, my clothes lying all over the
    floor—they had

that same color that they'd always had.

Every time I wanted a change of clothes my mom had to
    get out her wallet . . .

this time I could just . . .

pick some stuff . . . something I had worn before.

I didn't have to break anything in, I could just
    put something back on.

Which felt

really nice.

In fact, I put a few of my favorite old shirts on for
    the rest of the day,

just because I wanted to have something familiar on.

~

My neighborhood, mostly, is what really bothered me.

I, I had always liked the fact that my neighborhood
has just . . .

never been one of those neighborhoods that is
always jumping.

I mean, I remember for a while I was living in a hotel,

before I got to move back and, um,

it was right on Union Square, and it,

things were,

it's like, it's almost like—

it's kind of like a quieter Times Square but things never
slow down.

There are always cars, there are always people,

things are moving around and things are happening,
people have places to be.

Things *close* down here,

things stop, people . . .

I remember there were a few times in the past that I've
walked down the middle

of West Broadway,

after,

you know, coming home real late, just because I could.

And then, that was . . .

that was just gone.

# GOLDEN STATE

## Renée Levine, Building Coordinator

*Ms. Levine is a small, middle-aged woman with a no-nonsense
attitude and a sharp sense of humor. She wears a stylish blouse
and straight skirt, and has short, fluffy hair. She is clearly in
charge of an incredible number of things. She speaks with a
slight New York accent, and sometimes cuts off her words with
a sharp laugh.*

We've heard from maybe two hundred schools.
Not individuals—
we've heard from thousands of individuals.
But all of these boxes are still not open
with banners and cards and cranes,
and we've had an outpouring from
the world
with letters,
and I'm still not caught up with saying thank you.
Wishing us well,
people coming to visit,
there are beautiful banners all over.

~

And this young woman—
I got a call from California
that they wanted to bring a banner
and
I guess there is a Miss Teen America
or something
and this girl is Miss Cali—
Miss Golden State Teen
because she won some sorta pageant
and she came with her family.
We went into the conference room
and she presented
a banner
and we had some kids she could talk to
and she told us a little about the contest
and so on.
She had to have a talent.
It's like Miss America,
you know,
bathing suit
and, and, and . . . uh,
evening gown
and also

they had to have a platform.
You know,
something they wanted to do to help.
And her platform,
what she wanted to do to help,
was
to reach out
to
Stuyvesant and the people of New York
just
send wishes.
So
it was just a little bit of a . . .
I'm not used to seeing someone in a tiara
walking the streets of . . .
walking into Stuyvesant.
And um . . .
it was—
it was fun.
It sorta gave a little levity
to this whole situation.

We've just received
wonderful things.

If you go up to the library
there are books up there
that have been signed by
kids.
The banners—
you've seen the ones from Oklahoma City—
I mean,
we've received quilts
there are more quilts coming.
We must have . . .
do you know what a crane is?
The thousand cranes of peace?
I must have three thousand of them
which I still haven't put up.
But I will put them up.
I'm running out of space,
I'm running out of people to put them up,
I'm trying to get Kern all the time to help
um, but
he's in over his head.

It's just been heartwarming.
People are really . . .
I just got

during Christmas
(unfortunately)
three thousand Christmas cards
from a school in Utah
that the kids made.
I've gotten tapes, videos, CDs,
I still haven't looked at them.
It's totally overwhelming.

What we want to do now—
we think the other schools are coming back in
   the beginning of February
and we want to do something to welcome them back
'cause we're the only school back right now.
It's not your usual stuff.
It's just totally overwhelming
what people have done for us.
You can see this.
I thought I was caught up before—
you can forget it.
Every day something new arrives,
and it's *still coming.*
You're not going to find me in my office soon.

It's been very heartwarming.

People really do care

and we've become sorta famous.

Everybody knows Stuyvesant now.

And what I do to say thank you—

I have a letter that was signed by Jukay and Mr. Teitel.

We send a thank you letter

and a copy of *The Spectator*.

You know that quilt that's hanging

on the second floor here with all the sparkles?

That's so outstanding that we made them a plaque

to say thank you.

And we've gotten

um

a wonderful banner from Thomas Jefferson,

our sister school in Virginia.

They keep writing us to say they're thinking of us.

There's a beautiful flag in Mr. Teitel's office

that they presented us from Toms River.


It's just really heartwarming.

Shanleigh Jalea as Aleiya Gafar

# BIG KIDS

## Aleiya Gafar, junior, Big Sib/Red Cross Volunteer

*A short sixteen-year-old with a bubbly personality, Aleiya is a fast talker and speaks with energy and enthusiasm, especially when she starts talking about the firefighters and Red Cross donations. She stresses certain words, gesturing with her hands and sometimes pressing her fingers together. She tends to stand with all her weight on one leg and clasp her hands together by her waist when she's not using them. She wears jeans, sneakers, and a plain black long-sleeved shirt. As a Big Sib, she is responsible for helping a homeroom of freshmen ease into high school at the beginning of a new school year. It is clear that she cares about her charges.*

Normal?
Not really
considering we got back to school and
we weren't allowed out.
I mean
at the beginning, I understood why we weren't
uh, with all the checkpoints and

you know
all the police around
a-and all the hazardous material.
But now that we've calmed down, I really think that
we should be allowed to go out for lunch and—
you know, we don't need to walk around with our ID cards
    all the time—
who's gonna come into Stuyvesant that
that's gonna do something to us, and
the fact that they didn't want the alumni here
during Thanksgiving
I think that's really wrong because
do they think that our alumni pose a threat to
the Stuyvesant community?

I really think the freshmen reacted
a lot calmer than I thought they would
they even seemed to have the—the
situation more under control than some,
like, juniors and seniors that I know.
They
you know
talking to them after
you know, 9/11

they seemed kind of
disjointed from the whole thing because
I guess they weren't
here for
as long as
you know
most of us
and they didn't have like
the opportunity to go
you know, visit World Trade and shop there and
you know, just have the whole experience of it.
They haven't, like—
they didn't experience World Trade as
we know it, so I don't think they were as
affected unless
you know
they had family members that were lost.
I did talk to some of them and
the ones I talked to
you know, they were—
they were kind of—
that day, they were afraid because, you know
they're frustrated and
they just came to this school.

They hardly had, like, a full day of school and
this happened.
Um
you know, they were kind of
scared
going home
but
after that, and like after we went to Brooklyn Tech and
  everything
they—
they actually handled the situation with a level of maturity
  that I
didn't expect.


Well,
I mean I
called them and I talked to them and
you know, I asked them if they needed any help or
  anything.
You know, most of them were just like
"no, we're fine"
you know, they don't really . . .
they're big kids.

~

The day of

9/11, I went home.

I didn't even think about going to Red Cross. I really just
    wanted to make sure

everybody in my family was okay. And

even though

I did lose

my . . .

one of . . .

one of my aunts,

um,

like, I really didn't want to keep thinking about . . . uh—
    she was missing and

you know, we didn't know where she was.


And the next day, Red Cross called me in the morning and
    was like, "Can you come in?"

And

I really didn't know if I wanted to—

if I wanted to stay at home, but I was—

I figured, you know what, I need to get my mind off

of everything.

I need to do something.

I felt really, like

helpless

just staying at home.

And so

I decided to go to Red Cross and

we opened up the shelter at Shea Stadium.

There were firefighters and police officers, too,

you know

like a rest spot to eat, and

to sleep

and to have hot showers and

you know, new clothes

and

you know, every day

we were there and

y-you know, they'd say, like

three hundred firefighters would be coming and

the truth was

three hundred firefighters didn't come because

i-it—Shea Stadium is in Queens and—

and none of the firefighters or police officers really wanted to leave their area—

you know, leave Manhattan and come all the way to Queens.


We did get a group of firefighters from Ohio

from Brooklyn, Ohio,
and Parma, Ohio, and they were really great.
Um
some of them were really cute! *[Laughs]*
They were—
they were amazing people.
I mean, you'd see them
come in with all their . . .
their gear and
you know, they're all dusty and everything, and you
you kinda make them feel better
you know, giving them a hot,
like, meal, and—
and giving them new clothes
and, you know
just trying to cheer them up altogether. And
they drove
like, the day it happened,
they all just got in their cars and drove down here
and I thought that was really, really amazing.

We also worked at
the Red Cross chapter, you know
collecting money

and donations, and
yeah—things like that.
The day it happened, people were so
willing to give.
They called in with anything and
basically that first night and like
the first day or so
we took anything.
And then
when the needs were
you know, kind of met,
we started asking people for certain things.
It would be . . .
it would be on the news, and then five minutes later about
five hundred calls would come in.
"Okay, we have this, this, and this
do you want it?"
and we're like, okay
drop it off here
and as soon as people heard that we needed it—
it would be there.
And the people really wanted to donate lots of blood
and now there are like
waiting lists for people at the hospitals.

~

It's just really amazing how
everybody pulled together and
you know
like, reaching others—
and
people donated a lot of money.
Checks were like
a hundred dollars
like, kids pulled together
their little
piggy banks, and
schools sent in money and it was . . .
it was amazing because
I was talking to one of the
managers at
the chapter, and he was like
we don't even have this much money
like, the money we collected this week alone we
didn't get, like
almost all of last year
which is really funny, but
in times of need
people do give.

Shanleigh Jalea as Matt Polazzo

# SPECIAL

## Matt Polazzo, Social Studies teacher

*A social studies teacher in his twenties, Mr. Polazzo is one cool dude. He's very laid back, with a kind of mellow energy that can turn manic when he teaches. His voice is deep, and he often gestures with his hands as he speaks, unless he's holding on to the straps of his backpack. He wears a solid green army jacket, a large backpack, and a huge pair of headphones around his neck. He walks with a bounce in his step.*

Everyone was pretty frantic.
And then I was just . . .
kinda going north on my bike and I—
I was trying to—
people were like
leading groups of kids
and, but . . .
I don't think that anybody from Stuyvesant wanted to
   catch a ride
'cause

for whatever reason

I couldn't find any kids that really wanted to go with me.

*[Laughs]*

And eventually

I was kinda biking up

um . . .

by myself, but I did kinda

go back and forth between groups of kids 'cause I had my
  bike.

The stupid thing I did, was on my way down

you know,

while we were evacuating the kids, once I got all my
  kids out—

to the first floor and they were all there

I went back up to the

third floor.

I felt like, "This is it.

We're gonna die."

I had to get my bike outta here, but I

I had—

I had it locked in the Social Studies office s-so that . . .

So I went into the Social Studies office and like

the whole building's empty
and I
unlock my bike and I
brought it down.
But it turned out to be a good thing because
I was like
the first person to get back home that day, you know.
So I biked up.
It was weird too, because
the further north I biked
the more normal the city got
and by the time I got to Washington Heights
you—I live on a-hundred-and-fifty-seventh—
you wouldn't even know that
anything had happened . . .
at all.

Well . . .
I mean
I guess
on the face of it, the gift bag was really nice.
I mean
anytime a
corporation gives you lots of free shwag, I mean that's . . .

*[Laughs]*

that's always a good deal.

Y'know, the actual substance of it—

none of it was really, I mean,

none of these gifts that I was given are gonna permanently change my life.

I mean, they kinda gave us Discmans, but they were kinda like

low-end Discmans, but, I mean

hell, I mean

it's a free Discman

who am I to

complain and, you know, it's fantastic.

And,

you know

the CDs and whatnot—

i-it w— it was really nice.

I mean, it was a very

thoughtful and caring thing for them to do.

So

I'm not gonna say like, I'm against it—

I think it was great, um . . .

ideally, the kids would've gotten them,

you know what I mean? Like

I gave

most of my stuff away to kids, you know,

I got like toys and action figures and products

like some weird, free popcorn.

A lot of it seemed like products that they were testing

you know? *[Laughs]*

Yeah . . .

we popped this popcorn and

you know, you expect a certain . . .

taste when you eat popcorn, you know, and it's like—

I mean it's *sweet*—it's like . . .

it's a little bit odd.


I had a script committee meeting and all my kids were there

and I gave away about

half the stuff in my bag

but I kept some of it, heh.

The bag itself is useful. I can use it to carry my laundry

down into the laundry room

so that's really cool.

It was just nice, you know.

I mean

I felt a little guilty like

"Did I really deserve this?"

You know? I mean like
I guess I was helpful and
you know
evacuating and
trying to get the kids out and
I guess relaying messages when I was on my bike
but, y'know we were kinda just leaving the building but
I kinda feel like
you know . . .
but it all worked out okay.
So
I guess it was nice,
I mean, you know,
it was cool, I-I think it was good.
And it's good P.R. for them too.
I mean, it certainly makes me
predisposed to wanna
buy their
products.
And I was one of the few teachers that got a blue bag
     instead of a black bag, so . . .
that was pretty special.
     *[Laughs]*

Chantelle Smith as Anonymous Female Dining Hall Worker

# TURNING POINT

## Anonymous Female Dining Hall Worker

*The anonymous female dining hall worker is middle-aged,*
*soft-spoken, and calm. She speaks with a mild Southern accent,*
*and pronounces the days of the week "Mondey," "Tuesdey," etc.*
*She wears her uniform: white blouse, navy blue skirt and*
*apron, black shoes, hairnet. As she speaks, she sits very still,*
*her hands clasped in her lap, her head tilted thoughtfully to*
*one side.*

I'm a school lunch helper.
I'm here by seven o'clock
and I help set up the breakfast for the kids
and after breakfast right on into the lunch period,
preparation for the lunches until 1:45.

I went to Brooklyn Tech.
We didn't have to take any food over there.
Finding a way how to get over there
was sorta stressful
but, I made it there okay.

And when we got to Brooklyn Tech
it was, um . . . a matter of adjustment.
Because our kids came in at 1:00 to 1:30
so we had to go there like—
maybe our regular working hours—
go there and
the other workers from Brooklyn Tech, they were still there.
So when we got there we was sorta waitin' 'til they move
  out . . .
preparin' while they were still there,
bopping up into each other
tryin' to prepare for Stuyvesant kids.
And they have a big kitchen there
and a big staff
and because they have a big staff, the locker room was
  unbearable.
*Ooh woo!*
So tryin' to get in and out while they gettin' out
was sorta stressful but, we got it done.
We were required to stay there until 6:30.

Our kids started eatin' at 1:45.
The last serving period was 5:15 to 5:30
so we were there until 6:30.

I enjoyed sleeping late in the mornings
because I didn't have to get up so early
but when we came outta there it was DARK.
It didn't dawn on us at first that it was 6:30 in the evening
    that we were leavin' there
but we got useta it.


Right after World Trade
that Wednesday, well, no one came to work.
Thursday and Friday we went to other schools
and then that Monday,
the following Monday,
all of the Stuyvesant workers were required to report back here
to feed the workers
in the area.
We had to come back here and feed the workers.
It was stressful
when we first started coming back down.
The air was not good.
Getting off the train, the air was smoky.
I wore a mask, but I don't know how much good did it do,
you know,
but I didn't get sick or nothing.
My eyes didn't tear or nothing.

But I am very much concerned.
I drink a lot of water and
I was putting stuff in for my throat
you know
to try to keep my throat clean
you know, with zinc lozenges.
I still am very much concerned, healthwise
but thankfully I don't have asthma or none of that,
you know,
thankfully I didn't get no headache or nothing like that.

Getting off the train, tryin' to come here
you need ID. We had to stop,
stand in line outside to get the proper ID
in order to get into the building.
And we were working twenty-four hours
round the clock.
Some was working from eight to four.
Some was working from four to twelve.
And some was working from twelve to eight.
Twenty-four hours
a *lot* of preparation
a lot.
They were comin' in pickin' up food

takin' it back down to ground zero
so it was round the clock
makin' sandwiches, preparing salads,
vegetables, hot foods, breakfast,
lunch, dinner
you name it.

One man, he came by and passed out some information
suggestin' what can help us to relieve stress.
What he suggested to me was not enough
because I am a religious person
and
I'm a Jehovah's Witness
and I found a lot of comfort
from the Bible
and by going to my meetings and praying—
I never prayed so much in my life—
and reading and reading the Bible.
That really helped me to cope with coming back here.
Getting up in the morning knowing I have to come back
   down to Stuyvesant
near ground zero . . .
So that helped me to cope
a lot

and I'm still reading and reading
because every time I read the newspaper
or I see pictures of it
I would just feel like breaking down and crying.

It brought a lot of people closer together
and a lot of people are still under stress
who are not dealing with it
and I know that.
I see that.
And . . .
this is something we will never forget
and we really shouldn't want to forget it
because as a turning point in our life
some of us will mark it as a good thing.
For others, again, they stressed out
which is sad
and my heart really go out to those who lost loved ones
    there.
They will never be the same
and I don't want to ever forget
so I be looking for a person like that to try to comfort them
to share the comfort with them
that I KNOW has comfort me.

# THIS TIME

## Renée Levine, Building Coordinator

*Ms. Levine begins thoughtfully. She has been Building Coordinator since the early 1990s, and oversaw Stuyvesant's 1992 move from its old building on East 15th Street to its new building in Battery Park City. In the spring of 1993, during Stuyvesant's first year on Chambers Street, the World Trade Center was bombed for the first time.*

In 1993 the bang was very, very loud.
I thought the chemistry people had done something stupid
   with an experiment.
This time
the bang wasn't as loud.

So I went downstairs to the first floor
because I *knew* from 1993
that the Secret Service was going to use this
as a triage center.
They had told us afterward . . .
there were meetings after '93 about if there ever was

anything that happened
Stuyvesant would be used as a triage center
so I knew they were going to use the gyms
and I knew
they were going to use the theater.
And at that point
when I went downstairs
there were people starting to come in from the outside
'cause they wanted to use the telephones.
I told our kids who wanted to use the phones
to come into my office
so that they could use the phones
but by that time
I don't think the phones were working.

And I brought people from the outside
into the theater.
There were some mothers with carriages
and I sent for people from guidance to talk to the people
who were fairly hysterical.
And then they—
there was an announcement:
"Everybody go to homeroom."
And I have a homeroom.

My homeroom is in the lecture hall.

And the Secret Service did come in at that point and said,

"Everybody out of the theater."

And so everybody who was in the theater from outside

came into the lecture hall

with my homeroom

and

there were mothers and babies there and

one of them said:

"Oh, I don't have any milk,"

and one of my kids

from my homeroom

said, "I'll go up to the cafeteria."

This was at ten o'clock, I think.

I don't even know

when the first building came down.

He went up to the cafeteria,

came down with milk for the baby and

then we needed some cups

and another kid went up

and got some cups from Mr. Satin's office

and then we were all in there

and the Secret Service did—

they did take over at that point and

then the announcement came to leave the building.
And my homeroom
who is—
they're juniors
but they're very noisy.
I have some football players but
they were wonderful.
The kids did not panic at all.
You know the lecture hall, there's an exit out on the other
    side.
The boys carried all the carriages out first
and let the mothers and kids and all those people . . .
they took them all out and then my kids went out
and then we all went out the back.
We were among the first because we were the closest to the
    north exit.
And then the police were outside there saying
Run.

At that point
there were some kids crying
and I told the kids
every kid that I saw
because I couldn't keep my homeroom together . . .

I said, "Okay,

I want you to hold someone's hand.

I don't care if you know them or not.

You need . . .

just hold hands with someone

and don't look back."

And I didn't look back.

And I do not remember the buildings coming down.

I think one of them came down while we were here because

    I did see the lights flicker.

And then we all just ran

down to Pier 40

and since we were one of the first groups to get there

I waited there

and I told the kids 'cause I—

from '93 I knew that the chances of getting transportation

    were going to be minimal

and I said, "If you live in Manhattan,

go home.

If you have anybody,

an office in Manhattan, uptown, walk.

You're gonna walk

and take somebody with you

from Queens, Staten Island, and Brooklyn.

Just take them home until things straighten out.
If you find a phone, call them
but stay with somebody."
And then other people and adults started to come and the
    kids started to disperse
and I guess around noon
most of the kids had dispersed
and then I started to walk towards Chelsea.
I ran into a bunch of boys on the way
and I said:
"Where are you going?
Are you all right?!"
They were together.
That was good.
And they said they were going to St. Vincent's to give blood
and I went with them
but by the time they got to St. Vincent's
at that time there was no way to give.
The line was three blocks long.
And I kept going without them.

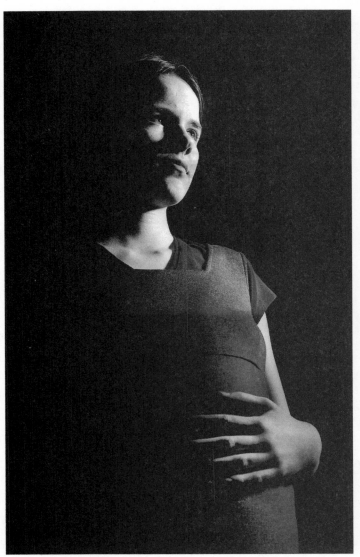

Anna Belc as Katherine Fletcher

# PRECIOUS CARGO

## Katherine Fletcher, English teacher

*Ms. Fletcher is thirty-one years old and nine months pregnant.*
*She touches her stomach as she speaks, resting her hands on it,*
*and sometimes presses the small of her back. She wears a simple,*
*straight maternity dress and comfortable shoes. She occasionally*
*pushes her bangs out of her eyes. Her voice is soothing, and*
*she speaks thoughtfully, taking time to choose her words.*
*Her emotions are level throughout, as is her tone.*

I think in times like that your . . .
you know, your instinct is to try to sort of
cling to
what's normal
I felt a great desire to remain,
to . . .
keep an atmosphere of calm
I felt a great responsibility to
show them an example of someone who was not going to
   fall apart
because I felt that if,

you know there's nothing scarier—
they're only thirteen and fourteen years old—
and there's nothing scarier, I think, than being in a
    scary situation and then seeing
that an adult who's supposed to be in charge is really scared
um . . . but on the other hand
I was terrified
I mean, you know, deep down I was . . .
I was terrified
and also, at the time, I was five months pregnant
and
I remember also just being very—you know, being very
    conscious of that
and I remember saying to my class, actually
you know, I want you to know that we're all perfectly safe
believe me.
I have very—
I'm carrying very precious cargo
and if I thought we were in danger I would leave
we would . . .
we would be leaving
and I said that even though I did feel . . .
I think I did feel in danger
because we had no idea what was going on.

~

There were days when I thought that maybe I would take a
   leave of absence
and I ended up deciding that
probably we're okay
and that I just sort of had to trust the way I felt
and the fact is that I didn't feel sick
you know,
it was very gross
and
smelled horrible
walking from the subway to school
but
I never felt . . .
I never had a sore throat
I never got a headache
um . . . you know, I felt fine
so I felt like that I sort of needed to trust that.

*[sigh]* Well . . . you know, it's funny because for the first
three months, I would say, after the attacks
so throughout November
you know, for all of September, October, November,
I felt actively sort of an active sense of fear every day

that I think everyone felt

and then one day I just sort of felt less afraid

but during that time of feeling afraid I felt like I was
     crazy to be in New York

and I know that

people who have children

especially

felt a strong desire, or considered, more actively than some,
     than other people, people who don't have children, um . . .
     considered more actively leaving New York

and I had lots of conversations with my friends about
     whether or not we would . . .

we would consider, you know, just completely changing our
     lives and leaving New York.

So far I don't know anyone who has done that.

But do I plan to raise my child in New York? Yes.

I love New York and um . . .

I don't believe that . . .

I believe that if my husband and my baby and I
     move to . . .

I don't know where we would go—

the country?

You know, maybe . . . actually, I think we would move to
     western Massachusetts if we were going to move to a

totally different life
but then, if you do that, what has happened is you really
    allowed your life to be completely defined by one event.
You know, I would always know that, you know,
when I was thirty-one years old
I had a baby and I moved to the country, and quit my job,
    and left my whole life behind because of this terrorist attack
and I think it's a really problematic thing to allow your life
    to be defined by one event.


I do think that people show each other . . .
well, I've always found New York to be a very friendly place,
you know, I feel like there's this weird myth about New
    York being really unfriendly.
I'm from Boston
and *Boston* is unfriendly.
New York is not unfriendly
you know, you always have sort of encounters with people
    on the street
and I've always felt that
the same way
like everywhere in the world, in cities, people really bond
    together when
something disastrous happens

like there's a blizzard

or a tornado

or

you know

when something big happens

then all of a sudden everyone is really nice to each other on
the streets or whatever

and I've always felt that New York sort of was in a constant
state of disaster

so there was always this feeling that we were sort of in
something together

and, in a way

New Yorkers are very well equipped to handle something
like what happened on September 11th

because we're used to feeling like we're in this sort of
state of crisis,

you know, it was just a much worse state of crisis
than normal.

I guess I do feel that

some people show each other more kindness

and

I felt like this year more people wished me a happy New
Year, for instance, than normal,

like cabdrivers and

people in stores.

You know, I believe that . . .
you know, I really believe in healing
and I believe that, the city will,
um . . . be
healed.
I think you have to believe that.

Liz O'Callahan as Hudson Williams-Eynon

# FACING NORTH

## Hudson Williams-Eynon, freshman

*Hudson is fourteen years old. His clothes—jeans and a T-shirt bearing a picture of Che Guevara—are a few sizes too big for him. He sits, slouched and cross-legged, with his hands crossed over his knees. When he gestures, he looks as if he is throwing his arms downward or flipping them away from himself. He stares straight forward when he speaks, and his words come slowly.*

Looking back on it, I shoulda been scared.
It was kind of like
I was scared
but then, like, it got,
I got like
y'know, I wasn't there.
It was all happening, like, way
away.
*[gestures away from himself]*
So I wasn't scared, you know?
Like, as soon as I was, like
done walking . . .

~

I guess now, like
people, like
every day
should just go
to the lunchroom,
go to lunch
and then
I always find the same people
sitting
where I was sitting.

My parents were like, y'know,
maybe I should transfer to Beacon
Which is probably where I would have went if I didn't go
    to Stuy.
I mean . . . I, I don't . . .
I don't really wanna go to Beacon
because like
I dunno, this is probably a stupid reason
and I'm just gonna look back at this and then, like . . .
but I dunno, it just feels like
I'd rather, like,
stick it out,
y'know? Like a challenge or something.

Everyone says
when you're young
you think you're, like, immortal or whatever
like . . .
*[pause, thinking]*

I felt that, like
I had objections to dissecting the worm
y'know, I would rather not
jus' kill an animal
just so that I can
learn about what's inside it.
So instead of dissecting the worm
I had to write like
a four-page report
on an earthworm.

I guess it's like that.
It's just like nothin's gonna happen to me, you know?
I kinda wanna stay, y'know?
I kinda like it.
So, yeah.

Marcel Briones as Juan Carlos Lopez

# SLIDE SHOW

## Juan Carlos Lopez, school safety agent

*Mr. Lopez keeps his arms folded across his chest and speaks congenially. His eyes are often fixed on the eyes of his audience, looking at them deeply. As he speaks, he tends to trail off, stuttering a little when the subject matter intensifies. When this happens, he rocks on the balls of his feet and gestures profusely to convey his ideas. He is dressed in uniform: dark blue slacks, light blue shirt, dark tie, dark blue uniform jacket with a gold-colored badge and a red, white, and blue ribbon pinned to it. He has a walkie-talkie in his pocket.*

I thought it was maybe
a single engine Cessna, or something
some small plane, an accident?
Yeah, right, pilot fell asleep,
had a heart attack, whatever,
any number of things and a small plane, you know
just a small dent
I thought
just a small hole, whatever.
It's like I-I-I couldn't believe

what I was seeing. And you know

I thought maybe because of the smoke and everything

from the first tower maybe

for some strange reason the second plane or something got
off course.

I thought it was just going to miss it or something

and it would just keep flying.


I got a call from my supervisor

to assist in evacuating P.S. 234 right over there on
Chambers Street

protecting children from collapsing towers

making sure they're not trampled by the onslaught of people

circumstances that ordinarily I wouldn't have to face

if it wasn't for these, these bastards

and ah, you know, I could think of other names to call them.

It's sort of like it just happened.

Young people are being so cavalier, you know,

the advantage of youth.

Young people have that ability to aspire to be

super men and women.

Young people are better able to have this sense

that . . . that

they're not as impacted.

I noticed that about a lot of young people:

they could smile, they could laugh, they could carry on as if
    nothing happened.
Then, you find out that you do have
human weaknesses
and, oh my god, I could die, and you are aware of your
    mortality
in other words.
For a little while I feared for my life.
I could have died that day conceivably, potentially,
you know, maybe not but there's a chance
anything could happen, exactly?
I got caught in that second cloud
by the collapse of that north tower
and I got grit and dust everywhere.


And, you know
what an odd thing this is
a peculiar little odd thing
just a little quirk, just
an odd thing but, ah, the day before
on Monday evening I had taken the time to shine my shoes.
'cause it's kind of weird I took the time to shine my shoes
and I did a good job, right,
and then Tuesday morning
it was a beautiful sunny day

you know
and as I was dusting myself off
from the debris of the north tower
I—I, I shook my clothes off and then I looked down
at my shoes and my shoes were a whole 'nother color
they were completely covered
and then I thought to myself
*I just shined them yesterday* and it was then this odd thought
just popped into my head,
this very peculiar thing,
it's totally absurd . . .
I thought for just a moment
if I had never shined my shoes
maybe this whole thing may never have happened.
As absurd as that sounds it sort of made me
laugh and cry at the same time. I called it my morbid
    moment.
If it was something as simple as that
then I would have never have shined my shoes ever.


I was always very patriotic.
I'm not a violent person.
Part of me felt like taking up arms and going to Afghanistan.
I'm a middle-aged guy . . .
if I could have, I would have.

This uniform, my authority, whatever

I try to exercise all of it well, but I wish I could do more.

You know,

I realized

whether someone was cutting class or not

wasn't as big a concern to me

as it might normally be

it's not like you guys are inmates

in some correctional facility of some sort.

I still see students as students.

I don't call you guys kids—

that's another thing.

I call you young adults, or ladies and gentlemen.

If I'm feeling upset,

I can imagine other people are feeling that way, too.

I try not to be overly officious.

I try not to be overly imposing

and if a person is caught cutting

I still tell him or her

to go to class please or whatever

and it's not time for that and it's not time for me—

I'm not looking to get anyone in trouble

and that's always been my approach.

I sometimes give a little lecture:

"We all have our responsibilities

you do yours and I do mine.
So get to class."
I don't keep a score of the number of people cutting
from day to day.
If I catch no one cutting,
I've had a good day.
I felt that I was more than
just a school safety agent,
I felt that not only that
but I was also serving my country.

I try to do normal everyday stuff,
but I'm not the same person I was.
It took me quite a while to sit down
and watch a movie without—
when I tried to distract myself,
I was too conscious that I was distracting myself.
Oftentimes I'd just turn it off or
I'd turn it off
and watch the news.
For the most part,
I need to know.
I can't not know, you know,
I try not to watch

but I can't not watch,
I just need to know what's going on
as many details as possible,
I got to work on this puzzle.

And ah, you know,
you know how they, they say your life
sort of flashes in front of you
and I always wondered about that.
I wondered whether it's a film on fast-forward
or what, what is it?
But you know, it's a slide show.
It's like a flash of photographs
in your head and you know
the last photograph in my head
and what would have been my last spoken word
was my son.
I pictured him in my mind
the last thing I ever thought I would utter in this world.
He lives with his mom.
We're going through some, ah, some post-divorce situations
that, ah . . . she's being very . . . selfish with him
so I haven't even really gotten
a chance to speak to him

or to ask him how he feels about what's goin' on
and to give him some insight or whatever?
I wish I could talk to him
about what's going on so
I could get his sense.
It made me go start in tears again and
I've been crying a lot since that day.
Right now, I'm tearing up a little bit
I need desperately to see my son . . .
I remember
that I would watch him
from the kitchen of my brownstone
I'd watch him play in the backyard.
I've had him for thirteen years, he's fourteen now.
I've seen and made a lot of sad smiles.


It's not a sense of hopelessness
but I think if it makes you feel hopeless . . .
if it feels hopeless,
then yeah I think, I think that person has lost everything.
You know I, I think at least bottom line
at least have hope
hope is everything . . . if nothing else have hope.
I hope I see or talk or whatever

with my son soon.
I hope they catch these knuckleheads,
you know, bin Laden and them.
We're this rich nation
you know
we're so decadent
and maybe we deserve this
even though we don't.
No . . . no.
Some of the interviews on TV
that we're so arrogant and that we deserve this
and whatever
I don't agree with that
no.
But anyways I hope this matter resolves itself soon
and it's gonna be a while.
I'm picking up the puzzle
pieces of my life
and putting it back together
and letting me see if this piece fits or that,
I need some sort of conclusion from
my ladies and gentlemen, the news,
my son,
then I could move on.

Taresh Batra as Katie Berringer

# EVERYBODY WAS A FRESHMAN

## Katie Berringer, freshman

*Katie is fourteen years old, extremely energetic, bubblier than you would think possible. She speaks quickly and with great expression, emphasizing those things that amaze and excite her—and there are many. She gestures furiously with her hands. As she speaks, she often stands with one hand on her hip, leaning all her weight on one leg. She wears tight jeans, a small T-shirt, and platform shoes.*

I wasn't really sure
as to how, like, a terrorist attack
was supposed to be like so
when they said "No one will be going to school tomorrow"
   I was like
"My brother goes to Bronx. Can't *he* go to school?"
When I told my parents we were going to Brooklyn Tech,
   my family was like
*Brooklyn . . . oooooh . . .*
My grandma called me.
My aunt in like North Carolina called me.

My grandma's friends all called me with like numbers
    of people
in Brooklyn.
Oh, and my other aunt was like "Oooh! I know a teacher at
    Brooklyn Tech
'cause she's like my best friend's daughter's like best friend
and like
here's her number!"
And I was just like do you really think I'm going to call a
    Brooklyn Tech *teacher*?

These people—
cuz like they were watching the news all the time
    and it was like
"These Stuy—these poor Stuy students in a ground zero
    high school are like
being relocated to Brooklyn Tech." *[in a deep voice]*
I mean *[laughs]*
and then I got to Brooklyn Tech and like, everybody was
    really mad! And like,
I was like, we have to go to Tech—that sucks, but HEY!
    One o'clock in the afternoon
is an o-kay time for me! *[laughs]*
But everybody was like "I wanna go to Stuy, I wanna go to
    Stuy."

And I was like have you *seen* Stuy

in the news?

Like there's *smoke* all around it.

I *really* don't think we need to go to Stuy right now.

But it was kinda weird

'cause it was only three days that I was at Stuy

and I was trying to develop SOME sort of system for
    getting to class

and at Brooklyn Tech I was like

what IS this whole north-south-west thing *[shakes head]*

but like . . .

you know,

in a way, it was kinda good cuz

everybody was like new, it wasn't like

"oh look at the stupid freshies"

it was more like "oh my god look at the stupid Stuy people"

you know *[laughs]* so *everybody* was like

"Where the hell are my classes?"

So it was kinda like everybody was a freshman

like, you know

the whole freshman thing.

Like I walked into the wrong class 'cause

I couldn't figure out the number system, but like

it was happening to everybody you know?

*[Slight pause]*

*[Smiles]* Also the thing was, like, in the sense that we
kinda took a break from what we were doing, you know
'cause like, teachers didn't wanna give you homework,
we had twenty-six-minute periods . . .
and like
all my classes started out with like, you know
"Write down how you are *feeling* today." *[laughs]*


But oh my lordie lu
the stairs!
I remember the first day
I walked up the wrong staircase and these Brooklyn Tech
    people
were like,
spitting at me, like "go the other way" and I was like
other way?
There's another way?
what is this stupid up-down stairs thing!


But Brooklyn Tech was all right, you know.


And then getting back to Stuy everyone was all excited
and like *Stuy*, thank *God*!
and I was like, does anyone else but me realize

that when we go back to Stuy

we have to wake up at *six in the morning,*

you know? *[laughs]*

Like am I the only one who thinks that?

Like, say good-bye to your late-night friends

you know

you have to, like, go to sleep early

and wake up early

and I was like "you people are stupid, like, forty-five-minute
   periods again!

You guys are *so* out of your minds."

Christopher M. Yee as Kevin Zhang

# HEARTLESS

## Kevin Zhang, sophomore

*Kevin Zhang is fifteen years old. His dress and speech reflect hip-hop culture. He speaks in a low tone of voice, sometimes gesturing like a rapper with his hands. He wears a leather jacket, jeans, and a platinum necklace, and spikes his hair.*

I went down to change my program.
It's on the second floor,
and then I—I saw something hit the . . .
building . . .
the first time.
I saw the whole thing, I saw something hit the building,
and then everyone was just laughing.
Everyone was laughing.

So,
I—I went back up to class,
and then the teacher was just teaching a lesson like nothing
    happened.
I was talking to some of my friends.

I was . . . I was asking if they saw the plane.
They're like "yeah" 'n' they were like, laughing,
    and it was like:
"This guy was blazed. This guy was just
totally stoned.
Some moron hit the building."

And then we went to Spanish class and then,
the second plane hit.
I actually saw a guy.
He threw a chair out the window,
and then . . .
That's when everyone started caring.
Yeah, before everyone was just thinking it was a joke.

They . . .
they were really heartless.
No, I'm serious,
they were just so heartless 'cause . . .
they were laughing after the first one hit and then
after the second one hit,
they were like, some of them started crying and stuff.
I'm saying,
"Why were you laughing then?

After the first one you know there's nothing to be
    funny about."

I know some people, they're like
"Well, that's just their luck,"
you know,
"Some people,
they have good luck and . . .
you know, they win the lottery and other people, they have
    bad luck and they get killed like this."

A lot of those people were my friends.
Or they're still my friend; I'm not gonna like
not be someone's friend 'cause they said something or
'cause they thinking one thing in one way but,
it made me think about them in a whole different way . . .

That's really horrible to say
'cause
all those people died and you just can't laugh it off it's not
    something you can laugh off.

For me I—I try not—
not to think about it too much.

'Cause we had a week off, every day I would just call up
    some friend,
or go see a movie or play baseball, play basketball, we'll just
do stuff that'll take my mind off of this,
you know.

My cousin was affected, too.
After a while . . .
he stopped partying for like a week.
'N' that's a really long time for him!
That was a *really* long time for him!

I don't think we'll ever be normal
again
after what happened.
It made me mature a lot emotionally.
It made me realize,
like,
the world's . . .
not what I thought before . . .
a lot more fucked-up people than I thought.

# YOU NEED HOPE

## Hector Perez and Haydee Sanabria, Special education students, P.S. 721

*Hector and Haydee are both students at P.S. 721M@Stuyvesant High School, a District 75 program for young adults with special needs that is housed in rooms on three of the top floors of Stuyvesant. The twenty-seven students at P.S. 721M are all developmentally delayed with cognitive challenges or a combination of cognitive and physical challenges. They are between the ages of fourteen and twenty-one.*

*Hector is nineteen years old, with a mild form of cerebral palsy that has paralyzed his left hand. He uses few gestures when speaking, and tilts his head slightly to the left. He speaks directly, but does not look straight at his audience unless he is vehement about something. He wears carpenter pants, a short-sleeved knit tennis shirt, and sneakers.*

*Haydee is seventeen years old. Her posture is confident, her voice powerful; she enunciates well, taking her time to make points until she has too much on her mind, at which point she spits out her words quickly, with a bit of a Hispanic accent. She is authoritative in her interactions with others. She dresses casually, in jeans and a T-shirt, and her hair is usually in a bun. She sings her first line.*

### Hector:

My name is Hector Perez.
I'm from the Dominican Republic.
I want to be a sports editor for some magazine.
I like to read.
Do I play? Yeah, I play a lot of sports,
ever since I learned to walk.

### Haydee:

*[sings] I'm a slave for you,*
that's my jam, yo.
I'm Haydee Sanabria.
I'm Puerto Rican and
I love to sing and dance.
When my moms ain't looking
I be, like, running,
running to the stairs place
of my apartment building so, so, so
I could sing as loud as I want to.
Britney
J. Lo

Shakira
What else do I do in the stairwell? I cry.


Hector:
A lot of people can walk
and they take it for granted.
The doctors told me
that I would never get to walk
because of my condition.
I worked real hard on P.T.—physical therapy—
and it hurt a lot, but not as much as what people say.


Haydee:
I cry in the stairwell
because I don't want my moms to hear me,
'cause then she starts crying too.
I live with my grandmother,
she's been my mother for
as long as I could remember.
My real mother died from AIDS before
I could remember what she looked like.
I just know people come up to me
and say I look just like her. But I don't mind 'cause
me, my grandmoms, my real moms all got the same name:

Haydee.

So it's okay when people say I look like Haydee—like me.


## Hector:

People look at me and
sometimes it's all in my head,
some pity, some smile and look away,
some make fun of me.
I decided a long time ago
if people don't want to get to know me
because they can't get over my disability
then it's their loss.
When people make me feel sad
I don't even want those people
to feel what I feel by making fun of them
so I turn the other cheek.
I play basketball, baseball,
anything that calls for two legs
cuz now I got them.


## Haydee:

My dad, my dad lives in the Bronx,
and he always be getting me stuff like video games,
I wake up early just to play them.

I like him and all, but he be introducin'
me to his girlfriends and I'll be like "Uh, uh!"
But, then he talks to me, tells me
how much he loved my mom,
how much he loves me.
He always provides for me,
I'm his baby. He's the only one
I could be me in front of.

Hector:

I was born in a wheelchair.
The doctors said that I'd die there, too
but you know
it's not in me to quit.
To be hopeless.
You need hope.
We need hope.
I remembered after the first plane hit
and no matter where you were
you could see the smoke.
I was with my friends and
our teachers were crying.
And I just tried to be strong for them,
to pray.

I prayed for me, too, for my dad
to pick me up and bring me home.
And there he was.
He said he ran to school
from Chinatown.


**Haydee:**
This stairwell is where I sing and cry
as loud as I want and no one could hear me.
Then, I go back to my moms,
and she be like, "Where you been?"
I look at her straight and
I say, "I just been places."
I don't need her worrying about me,
she did enough of that for my mom when she . . .
I don't remember my mom,
but I remember my grandma crying.


**Hector:**
Seeing it on TV made me want
to help out, do something.
I feel bad. No matter
how independent I want to be,
I can't think of a place
without moms and dads.

I got a big family, they got my back,
and I couldn't imagine them not there for me.

Haydee:
Yeah, it was loud and
everybody was running, screaming.
My brother goes to St. John's
so, I knew I had someone to take care of me.
Someone to take me home.
He's always been there
when people make fun of me
and call me slow.

Hector:
I cried a lot
for those families
who are hurting.
I pray for them every day,
I feel bad but
I know it's gonna get better.

Haydee:
When I got home
I started drawing like mad,
trying to remember

what the towers look like
before I forget.
And I took my favorite one
and hung it up on my wall
and I got Christmas lights around it
white Christmas lights
and I just looked at it until I fell asleep.

Hector:
I don't like it
when people treat me differently
better or worse
just because of this.
I want people to see me
the me
who does not want to be pitied
or pegged useless.
Ignorance hurts.

# A VERY INTRIGUING TRAIN

## Eddie Kalletta, sophomore

*Eddie is fifteen years old. He uses his hands when he talks,*
*gesturing quickly and emphatically, and speaks rapidly in a*
*high-pitched voice. He is extremely energetic, walking from*
*place to place as he talks; even when he stands still, his hands*
*are moving. He sometimes leans all of his weight to one side*
*of his body as he speaks. He wears a green sweater, khakis,*
*and boots.*

You know so it,
it wasn't quite . . .
like sophomore year wasn't quite as good as I thought it
    was gonna be even though it was only the third or fourth
    day of school.
After school, around four o'clock, I was leaving.
I always wanted to take the Q train—it was a very
*intriguing*
train for me.

The Q train, it goes by Kings Highway and there's

a Kaplan there, you know, the

college test prep course or whatever.

And I was like, "Oh, you know

I think I'm gonna go there after I go take the PSATs or
   whatever junior year so I can do good on my SATs."

And this woman next to us she turned around and she was
   really friendly, she was like

"You know,

I took Kaplan and it was terrible, I ended up studying out of
   my friend's Princeton Review book, so I did well" or
   whatever.

And I was like "thank you very much" and it was just so
   weird for someone to be

*so friendly . . .*


So I get off the train and all of a *sudden* I realize I have
   no idea where I'm going.

The ferry leaves this time, this time, and this time and I had
   just missed

*that* ferry. *[gesturing]*

So I go down to where the ferry was supposed to be,

and it's like abandoned except for this one like

Russian guy who, like, I ask him

"Was there a ferry here?" and he's like "no speak English"

you know, so I was like
*"okay . . ."*

All of a sudden,
the heavens like . . .
break loose, and it just starts pouring.
I had to run
down like three blocks
and I was next to this one kid who was just getting *off* work
and this like war vet
with like one leg.

So I called my mom,
and like there was no way I was gonna get home so
my dad came and bailed me out and he picked me up.
I remember being in my room around nine o'clock,
and I was like, "You know, today was a bad day."
And my mom was like:
"Don't worry, tomorrow will be a better day."

And that was September tenth.

# INTERMISSION

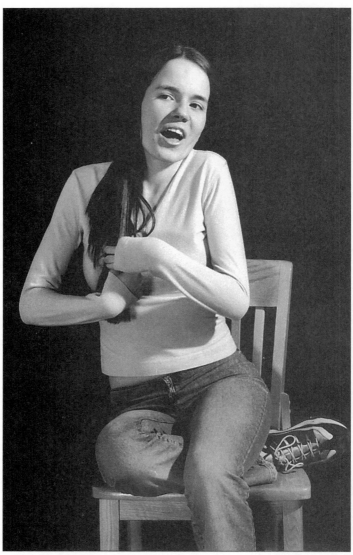

Anna Belc as Mira Rapp-Hooper

# Act Two

## THINGS BELOW, THINGS ABOVE

### Mira Rapp-Hooper, senior

*Mira is seventeen years old, extremely energetic and bouncy.
She sits on a chair with one leg tucked up under her. Her hair
is long, and hangs loose down her back. As she speaks, she plays
with it, pulling it behind her with both hands, winding it
into a loose bun, then letting it fall again. She shifts her torso,
leaning her head from side to side; she is never entirely still.
She wears tight jeans and a tight long-sleeved shirt, and plays
with the cuffs of the shirt, hiding her hands as she speaks.
Her speech is rapid and enthusiastic, her tone upbeat.
Genuine happiness shines through starting with the line,
"Once we . . . everyone was so happy and smiley . . ."*

I went to
all those vigils that happened in Union Square right
  afterwards and it was just the most amazing experience.
  Like, it gave me so much faith in New York.

I was almost more,

like, nostalgic,

but optimistic

and hopeful

and

forgiving

and trusting of people than I ever would have thought
    anyone could be in this situation.

And I don't know, it was just everything that was missing
    from New York was suddenly back there again.

And . . . before . . . I was always thinking:

*Oh, I'm leaving for college, I'm never coming back here, like,*
*I'm gonna move to a nice,*

*clean city where everybody likes each other.*

And then after this I just realized that like no matter how
    far I go I always have to come back here because

the feeling that I've gotten within the last three months
    has been an irreplaceable one.


Every time I walked down Sixth Avenue and saw the

empty space, I would start to cry a little bit.

And every time I saw someone with an American flag

I would feel a little bit better.

I'm not like a

major nationalist or anything.

It's not even—
it doesn't mean nationalism to me
to me it means like
spirit and
like pride in—not necessarily just your country—
but pride in yourself as a person and as a community.

In the flag ceremony,
I chose to be the United States
which was a lot of fun.
Everybody who carried all the flags was
awesome and everyone was really into it so it was a really
    nice ceremony in general.
I was very happy that I got to
kind of represent America,
partially just because I . . . I don't really identify with
    any other nation.
I'm a mix of everything so I couldn't have really attributed
    myself to anything besides America but it felt really good
    to be able to kind of
think to myself,
even if only to myself,
that I was like some part of the American spirit,
whatever that is.

~

I didn't really get to see

the speakers and stuff because they lined the flags up

in alphabetical order and I was U

so I was all the way over there.

But I know the mayor was there and I know he did

a really good job 'cause that's what people said.

The part about the ceremony that was so good for me

was just

like

everybody

being together in the ceremony and everybody

genuinely wanting to do it and nobody was forced into it.

Like,

people volunteered their time to be part of this thing

that involved us walking all the way down

to the Battery in the freezing cold

and carrying these huge flags because

they wanted to be a part of this

uniting of

everyone who had been affected by it and I don't know

if people looked into it

that much and

that ideologically but people wanted to represent

their countries and people wanted to be a part of something

that had affected them as a school.

And I think that it meant a lot to people that we were
   asked to carry the flags just because
there has been a lot of recognition about the school
but this is a little bit more that
we were so close that we deserved to have a hand in this
because we were
a part of it too. And
we were helping to commemorate
the people who have been lost
and it was just—
it was really beautiful.
Once we . . . everyone was so happy and smiley and
even though it was
a
sad
thing
because
we were commemorating
three months
after September 11th
it was a really nice occasion just because
the park was so nice and
it was beautiful and
we put up our flags and there were just these eighty-two
   flags going around

this dent-

type thing

in front of a garden.

And it just reminded you that like regardless of what had
    happened like half a mile up

there were still beautiful things below

and beautiful things above

and before long there would be beautiful things there too.

And it was—

it was just a good feeling to have everybody together

and have

everybody commemorating the event without

having to be so sad,

with hope

and with remembrance but . . .

and again with hope and optimism

for what was to come.

And not

a negative attitude about what had happened

but more of a positive attitude about what would happen.

# SAFETY NET

## Max Willens, senior

*Max is still in baggy pants, sweatshirt, and glasses. He is seated in a coffee shop, but does not speak any more quietly than he might outside on the street. He begins with a punch, almost spitting out the first section with annoyance.*

There were people there *all the time,*
and they weren't even New Yorkers,
they weren't even people visiting some, you know,
taking a look at something that used to *be* there,
something that they used to know.
They were people from Kansas and Oklahoma, and,
    you know,
Missouri, who had seen those places on postcards.
And they wanted to buy hats and pins,
and wanted to sing "God Bless America" and things
    like that.
Which made me sick.

The pictures,

the pictures were probably what really did it for me.
There were these disposable cameras,
the kind that people, you know,
whip out for trips to Disneyland or the Grand Canyon,
   you know,
those yellow plastic things, you know,
where everyone crowds around and the flashes make those
   little annoying
yellow sounds.
And I had to, I dunno . . .
one time, someone actually asked me to take a
   photograph of them,
of them looking,
kind of standing in a solemn pose with the wreckage as
   a backdrop,
and I couldn't do it.
I nearly threw the camera at them, I just . . .
I couldn't . . .
It made me sick.

I remember for a while I had this,
this retort worked out in my head where—
I'd even rehearsed it a few times.
Back when it really made me mad.

I would throw the camera back into their . . .

back at them, you know,

maybe even into their face and say,

"The next time someone blows—someone blows up

   something very important to you

in your backyard, I'll be sure,

be sure to take the photos that I want to pose in.

I'll be sure to ask you to take them."

I dunno.

I remember cursing a lot in them,

those little monologues that were supposed to be delivered

   to those little

people.


There's an observation deck on Broadway and Barclay.

The fact that there are people staring at a tomb of

   three thousand *people* . . .

the wreckage and the rubble that's awesome enough in

   and of itself.

*[pause]*

So much to look at.


I—

I'm reluctant to give the "I appreciate everything

so much more" speech.

I'm not

I am

I'm almost

kind of

more upset with . . .

the country that I live in,

now than I was . . . um . . .

I guess . . .

prior to the attacks I remember,

a lot of people—my friends, you know,

a lot of my peers had this kind of cynical "the dollar
   drives America" ideas

in their heads,

and I thought that,

I thought that it was true but I thought that

if something truly *awful* happened or

if something truly *meaningful* happened, that they'd calm
   down and behave like,

I guess,

like sensible people.

But after this,

I realized that

that's not true.

That, you know,

like a month after this had happened,

there were all these patriotic car ads on television,

people were like . . .

Like Chevy was claiming it was being a good American
   company by offering

zero percent financing on its latest truck.


It seems to me that if you were an American before you're
   an American now.

You know, our freedom is still here, they haven't taken
   that away.

They just—

they attacked us because . . .

because they disagree with us,

and they killed a lot of innocent people.

And that's what people should be upset about—

they shouldn't be upset about attacks on freedom,

they shouldn't be upset about attacks on "our way of life,"

they should be upset that . . .

a lot of friends, a lot of children,

a lot of, you know,

a lot of people's sons and daughters,

a lot of, you know,

fathers,

and mothers,

have been killed, and a lot of, you know,

some families now no longer have a provider,

some people don't have houses anymore,

you know,

and *that's* what we should all be mourning.


I think school's okay.

I think that—

I think that actually,

for the first time in a really long while,

I've looked forward to—

to the social opportunities of being around a lot of people,

that I can speak to.

It's not even that I do, I don't,

I've never—I've never brought the 11th up in school with
    my friends,

I've never discussed it except maybe in a political context,

but, just having these people,

just being able to walk around realizing you're kind of in

a safety net, or you're right next to one,

is very reassuring.

I mean going home and being alone has never been . . .

And it is alone really.

Because you're with your mom who's dealing with
her own . . .

who's dealing with it herself by just talking it to *death*
every time we have

people over or we go over to people's houses.


She has like a list of things she tells people,

first there's the story of how she got the dog out

and then there's the story of how we had to stay in the hotel

and how we had to move from house to house and then
there's the story of, you know,

why, the, the repression in Afghanistan like,

caused this all to happen.

And there are these stories that I can almost time them,

it takes about an hour and a half for her to go through it,

pretty much,

if you allow for about ten to fifteen minutes of
other people injecting their

little thoughts on it.

It takes about an hour and a half for her to
get her thing out,

and it happens every time and I'm sick of it.

But that's how she deals with it.

And then in the end, when I run out of homework

and I run out of, you know,

distractions to find,

all—all that's really left is thoughts that I haven't really,

that I don't really want to wrap my head around.

And there are, you know,

and there are things I don't think I can or want to come to

terms with yet.

Or I don't even know if I'm supposed to be able to . . . I . . .

I mean . . .


I remember when I was—how old was I?

I guess I was fourteen, and I wondered about . . .

I figured every generation had something that they

remembered,

every generation had something,

when they were growing up, when they were coming of age,

there was something bigger than them that they had to

deal with

that they had to grow up around,

or grow up,

or grow up through.

And I was kind of wondering,

cuz in those days we were, like,

riding high on this wave of economic boom and

everyone was, you know,

making money, and everyone was, you know,

buying new things and getting happier and happier

   all the time and I thought,

we won't have a great war,

I don't even know that I want one,

but we won't have a big breakthrough,

we won't . . . we won't have a great piece of adversity to

   overcome.

I guess I was wrong, but,

I'm surprised that . . .


*Max is cut off by a man sitting at an adjacent table in the
coffee shop. This anonymous man is middle-aged, with a
ponytail and glasses. He wears khaki pants and a gray cardigan
sweater. He has a huge black duffel bag at his feet out of which,
as he speaks, he takes seemingly random art supplies (a pad,
colored pencils, pens), which he never uses. He speaks in a high
voice that squeaks when he becomes particularly animated or
excited. His hands are almost always at right angles to his arms,
whether in or out, making his wrists appear floppy. His legs are
crossed with one knee directly atop the other.*

Tim Drinan as Anonymous Coffee Shop Man

**Anonymous middle-aged man in coffee shop:**
You weren't wrong.

**Max:**
Yep. I was.

**Anonymous middle-aged man in coffee shop:**
You weren't.

**Max:**
I wasn't?

**Anonymous middle-aged man in coffee shop:**
Nope.
All those things you talked about, that people want
   to do.
This didn't need to happen.
The disparity, the discomfort around the world is absurd.
There's, there's an old old plotted course, and nobody gives
   a fuck.
And the fact that, you know,
people don't have the intelligence and the consciences,
is tragic. But,
that, well why, why aren't you?

You're an intelligent person. I'm assuming you go to
   Stuyvesant.
You gotta put that in perspective, you know.
Thirty-five hundred people died today in the Congo,
died yesterday.
September 11th, thirty-six thousand
children starved to death.
I mean, you know,
everything was hunky-dory here till that happened.
Cuz our values are twisted.
Ha ha, that's the reality.
That it's global.
This is a global thing,
and . . .
not that you really have anything to do with it,
but, you know, as you . . .
get more access to information,
and resources . . .
You know, you want to be a part of it.
It's not that you're, you know a bad guy or anything.
But you know,
the internet,
there's a global capital.
Which is basically what the deal is.

Forty-five people have fifty percent of the wealth in the
    world.
And you know,
because now the corporations are now conglomerating,
it's absurd,
and they don't give a fuck.
You know, a tiny example is Enron. You know,
how low can you get?
These guys sold out . . . they cashed out their chips,
and they sold their stock to their own workers,
knowing that they were gonna crash.
To their own *workers*?
You know, you're talking about millionaires—
the people who elected our president.
So, you know,
that's the deal,
it's really a real loss.
This money obsession is basically the deal.
Money is basically the deal.
The haves and the have-nots.
The history of this country,
relative to racism,
still has not been solved . . .
but if it was more of an equal distribution . . .

~

I teach Chinese kids that just came over.

And I teach American teenagers too.

There are all kinds of assessments.

So basically, the average kids are thrown out.

But, you know,

your system, my system—our system—I'm a Stuyvesant

graduate too—

it's just . . .

The hierarchy doesn't allow for much change at the bottom.

I'm wound up too, and, you know

It's very difficult for me, because, you know,

I try to change the way we do things.

But these alternative schools,

even they refuse to allow us to do anything.

Everyone, you know,

they're afraid to stand up.

You know,

they don't realize what's about to happen. You know.

So, we're talking about a lot of people.

So . . .

it happens to be a considerable population.

We're talking about a million people here.

*[pause]*

When you vote, by the way . . .

Giuliani,

the World Trade Center notwithstanding,

what he did in eight years

was basically criminal.

He basically tried to destroy the system,

which is absurd.

You know, you can't undermine the teachers,

whatever their competence is.

We need to teach the young people certain things if they
want to come into

this world, ha ha,

and we're just . . .

not doing that, you know?


Well, that's my cynical lecture for the day, ha ha.

Alright, fellas?

Be well.

I wish you guys luck.

So, take care now.

Catherine Choy as Owen Cornwall

# TENDER LOVIN'

Owen Cornwall, senior

*Owen is seventeen years old, with a reddish complexion and blond hair. He slouches as he sits, bent forward slightly over his stomach. He is extremely relaxed, and speaks in a deep voice. He wears khakis, brown shoes, and a dark patterned sweater. As he speaks, he pushes his sleeves up regularly. He makes great eye contact.*

It has been a bit ridiculous . . .
*[sincerely]* but I think everyone's had to have their cries and,
    you know, get some stuff out.

But I think the major disorder . . .
I just noticed, like,
it was almost impossible to have conversations
cuz you know you just couldn't CATCH
the conversation.
People couldn't focus.
It was this stream of ideas.
And that was . . . that was almost driving me crazy.

But I think for a little while I think people felt bad . . .
they couldn't . . .
just talk to people about THINGS.
People couldn't just shoot the shit . . . so to speak.
It was a bit . . .
difficult.

I think I've been spacing out lately.
And I don't know
sometimes . . .
I
lack motivation
to talk to people.
Or
you know
I just don't have the energy, you know,
the emotional energy.

There was definitely a problem. *[matter of fact]*
Some days you'd think about it a lot and
just feel sorry for yourself.

I needed
some

tender lovin' . . .
I think from my family.
I think it was good cuz I'm close with my family.
My mom's a bit of an anxious person
and I'm just naturally . . .
my demeanor is
a little bit more
chilled out.
We were both stressed out . . .

I think there's just so much uncertainty . . .
like sometimes I don't wanna go home.
And my home's the perfect place to go—
there's NOOO reason for me to not go home.
Sometimes I just wanna chill with my friends . . .
I never felt that way before.
And sometimes I just wanna go home and not talk
   to anyone.
Sometimes
I just don't know where I stand.

Christopher M. Yee as Eddie Kalletta

# WAKE-UP CALL

## Eddie Kalletta, sophomore

*Eddie is still in green sweater, khakis, and boots. He begins
speaking while seated, rises from his chair when describing the
events of November 12th, then returns to his seat, slightly
subdued.*

I think,
at least for me, when it first happened,
the first thing I said to myself was *"Okay,
this is the wake-up call for you and the rest of the world this is
    when you're gonna start living each day to the fullest"*
blah blah blah . . .
it doesn't happen!
It really doesn't!

You know you still don't tell all the people
all you want to tell them,
like you're still holding back from saying certain things
    to certain people
you know . . .

you still don't live life without regret, you know,
    you still . . .

Like, my philosophy on life hasn't changed so much,
    I'm not like "*oh,*
now let me go out and party and you know, live life
    to the fullest."
'cause that's what I wanted to do, really just enjoy life
    as much as I could 'cause you know,
you never know when it's going to end and
I was busy you know spending
all my time with books
and, you know
schoolwork.

I don't know if . . .
have you ever been to Rockaway?
It happened on a Monday morning, you know,
    Veterans Day.
I was just really starting to *heal*
from the attacks . . . I was really starting to
move on with my life.

If I looked out my window,

I could see where those houses stood.

It was probably around eight o'clock, you know,

I wake up like "agh, I wanna go back to sleep."

So I was . . .

I was lying in bed and, ah . . .


I guess it was like 9:15

I hear a plane.

This is *all* within like a thirty-second time span,

you know.

I was lying in bed and like

I was in this weird position in my covers and I said to
    myself, "Eddie,

*don't* look out the window whatever you do,

*don't* look out the window."

It just got . . .

*U-unbearably* . . .

the *worst* sound you could ever hear in your life it was
    the most

*loudest* . . .

*insane* like *moaning* thing and all of a sudden . . .

there's a bang and then . . .

the most gigantic *roar* you've ever heard like a

**PPHOOOOSH!!!**

~

We ran out onto the street and like . . .

as soon as the plane crashed,

in a way I was just . . .

I was wondering if the wall was about to come
  caving down on me.

I figured, "Wow, maybe you know, this is it for me,"
  you know.

I was just like "Wow, am I about to die," you know,
  it's the strangest . . .

*weird* feeling . . .


The plane flattened . . .

three houses . . .

but um . . .

you know . . . *[sigh]*

I mean it's j— it's just really weird and I still haven't
  gotten used to the fact that that's . . .

happened . . .


I think that September 11th . . .

*thus* far in my life that was the most, you know

pivotal event in my life, that was the most pivotal event
  like ever in the world, you know.

We were there
you know, for this,
but *I* was *there*, for
the plane crash.
And you know sometimes you feel like you're unlucky
    'cause all this stuff has happened to you but then you
    know
*I'm lucky*
because
it could've been *me*, that could've been my house it just
    landed on, you know.
The um,
the plane in Rockaway . . .
this is—this is my block.


And um . . . *[long pause]*
You know it—it's a lot more personal—it's so *close*
    and like . . .
I'm . . .
I'm forever thankful that I didn't look out my window
    that day.

Shanleigh Jalea as Jukay Hsu

# POWERLESS

## Jukay Hsu, senior, Student Union president

*Jukay is seventeen years old, Stuyvesant's Student Union (SU) president. He is also a youth chairperson for a Red Cross chapter in Queens, a position which allowed him to visit Stuyvesant shortly after September 11th. He can be a soft public speaker, and tends to drag his words and slouch a little as he speaks. He shrugs his shoulders and gestures faintly with his hands throughout. He wears a bright orange long-sleeved T-shirt and loose, but not too baggy, jeans.*

Well, I visited the site on one day
and
it was horrible.
I wish I didn't come.
And it's not because of
like, horrific scenes or anything, but
you really feel useless
because
there's nothing you can like—
there's nothing I . . .

I could do.
I wasn't old enough, like, I—
I'm not a fireman.
I wasn't old enough. I can't go pick up debris.
So . . . and you know there was—
the school was being used as like a . . .
triage and
you know, food house and everything like that
but
they had more than enough people to help out with the food
you know, preparations and things like that.
So it felt like
I was
taking up space and getting in the way of
emergency workers and the firemen and policemen
that were actually, you know
going in and like
helping find—
you know—
rescue people
and helping move the debris.
And that's the way I felt
so . . . um . . .
yeah.

And just like

coming here and leaving

is *impossible* because

the whole street was filled up with

with cars

and like, you know, supply trucks

and buses

and you just couldn't get out.

I mean, we got lucky.

We got in because like . . .

I dunno.

Someone from Red Cross knew

like . . .

we were with DEA people or something and they had
  the little

uh, um . . .

siren things?

So

we kind of cut past everyone to clear the way. *[Laughs]*

Yeah.

But leaving took *forever*.

Like

it was just a disa—

like, yeah.

I didn't wanna stay here.

Also

there was like, constant pressure because

I mean

every day the situation changed and there was just . . .

meetings like

every day before school

at Brooklyn Tech

and during school.

I missed like, half of my classes because of it.

I mean *[laughs]*

'cause we're

trying to come up with all these contingency plans

on how we can improve Brooklyn Tech

the students

and how we can move back to school

and how to make it as best as possible.

Since like, the situation was changing every day

all of our efforts that we came up with every day

like meeting with

Mr. Blaufarb and Mr. Teitel

they basically had like, meetings

throughout the day, and

the next day

everything changed.

So then we had to start from basically scratch.


And a lot of the things . . .

I mean

the Board of Ed was just very uncooperative with us.

Um

like they wouldn't

you know, they wouldn't tell us the test results,

they wouldn't tell us this and that.

It just seemed like they were

kind of

ruining everything that, you know

that we're trying to do

and

that made it very difficult, but . . .

I mean, yeah.


Th-the most important thing—

the most difficult thing was just trying to figure out like,
   everything—

like what was going on

and how to best like

help

the situation.
'Cause I mean . . .
even as SU pres—

It was just frustrating to see like—
"Okay, so what can I really do?"
You know, to help the situation?
And the only thing like,
that I could come up with was to, you know
to warn people as best as possible
through e-mails, whatever
like
what I knew of what was going on.
And
other things like
well, people have stuff in their lockers
and you know
different things that people wanted me to do.
You know—
try to think of situations like
maybe we can
get someone to come into the school
or like
I could come to school and get the things.

But then we kept—
everything kept getting frustrated by, you know
either the administration, or
most likely
the Board of Education—
because like
"it wasn't safe here"
or this or that.
So
it feels sort of . . .
I guess powerless?

I wish I could've done more
but
everything that we, we did and we tried to do
with us and the administration
it just . . .
was basically worthless—
a waste of time . . .
because it just kept changing.
It was a lot of like
bullshit
politics.

Chantelle Smith as Anonymous Male Custodian

# I LIVE MY LIFE HERE

## Anonymous Male Custodian

*The anonymous male custodian is middle-aged, with laugh lines around his eyes. He projects a tough, jocular exterior, but as he speaks his emotions become clear. He wears a Mets T-shirt, jeans, and sneakers, and speaks with a Long Island accent. He holds a large broom in one hand, occasionally leaning on it and grasping it with both hands.*

It was amazing how much
stuff there was going on and how quiet it was
ya know
and I account that to the dust
which was like snow
ya know what I mean
like it took all the sound in
and wasn't bustling, wasn't crazy noise
was more like sedated
and ah . . .
I don't think anything prepared me for getting out of the
    truck.

Ah . . . I guess
we got out right up here
I don't know what this street is, ah—
Canal Street, ya know.
The truck had to make a left
and we were like that's our building right there
that's where we're going
and when I got out
I was like yo, nothing prepared me for that, nothing
ya know I live my life here
this is nine hours a day I live here
and I never thought
never in my million years . . .
and I'm gonna cry, and I don't wanna cry all the time.
I been cryin' a lot
ya know what I mean
that's why I couldn't sleep last night, cuz you brought it up
   again and I thought what am I gonna say to her and it like
totally freaks me out
ya know.

In the nine years I've been here
I've been in charge of keeping that damn floor shiny and
ya know

keeping everything beautiful

and it was just like a, ah . . .

a rigmarole

or a, ah . . . cluster-eff . . . if you would.

Ya know what I mean

it was like everybody was movin' and you were like what the
   hell is going on here

ya know what I mean,

this is crazy,

ya know

but it was so organized after you stepped into it

it was like okay this is pretty organized,

we know what the hell is going on

and then, ah . . .

I'll never forget I saw the day crew and they were here since,

ya know for over twenty-four hours

and ah . . .

and it was nice to see 'em

ya know.

Because you didn't know what kind of a pile two buildings
   made

ya know what I mean

you were like, oh my god, ya know

how big of a pile does it make?

I remember sittin' at home thinking that.

Going *Is my building there?*

Is the pile up to the doors? Is it . . .

ya know

so I never really—

ya know

and then I saw them

and I was like okay, this is pretty good.


We had some light ya know

I could see by the lights that we were on emergency generator

ya know

and ah . . . the toilets weren't working or anything for the
   whole time until I got there

and just as when I got there they got them up and running

then we had to unclog all that.

And ah . . .

I'm not the kind of person that cleans up dog shit in my
   backyard

ya know what I mean

I puke.

When my wife wanted a dog I told her she had to clean it up

cuz I can't do that.

I throw up.

I can change my babies' diapers

because they're my babies, I guess

I don't know

ya know

but ah . . . dog shit I can't clean up.

And I went in there and said oh my god why'd you do this
to me

it is the only thing that you really could do to me that
would really affect me the most

was these piles of crap!

ya know

and I was like oh my god

ya know

and when I got that done I was like wow!

Ya know that's got to be the worst thing that could happen
to me

and then I realized there was so much more to do here

and everywhere you looked there was just another thing to do

ya know, it was like, ah . . .

in fact at one point it was like, you can't get in the building

there was so much supplies piled up outside

it was like blocking the entranceway.


I remember blankets and pillows; anything to do with sleep
went to the third floor.

It was, like, "Put everything on the third floor that's for

sleeping," ya know
the second floor was clothes ya know
and then ah . . . the fifth floor was all food ya know
and that's the way we started
and ah . . . it just kept getting out of hand with more stuff
    kept coming in.
It was unbelievable.


But I don't remember a lot about the first three days
to tell you the truth
cuz I was here for three days straight
ya know
in those three days . . .
I slept maybe an hour
and that was
ya know
because I was sorta forced to lay down
ya know people said I'm losing it
he's gotta lay down for a minute
or an hour
felt like three days but it was an hour
ya know
but that's all you needed.

~

Those three days had such high highs
ya know and such low lows
cuz I really thought
ya know, there was gonna be people alive
when I showed up I was like, we're gonna get people out
ya know, and that's why I'm here and that's what I want
   to do
*and it never happened* ya know
so that bothers me still, ya know.


And I remember on the first day like makin' eye contact
   with everyone
I don't know where you're from—
you're from the city so you know—
you don't make eye contact when you're walkin'
but this was the only way you communicated for the first
   couple of hours was
everybody had masks on
everybody was looking at each other
and I was like this is amazing
ya know.


But then it got more political and more political
and I was just like

ya know
people down here shaking hands
and ya know
I was like that's not what it's all about.
I don't really need a handshake from the chancellor.
I don't know who he thinks he is
or ya know what I mean,
it wasn't about you, it wasn't about
Rudy Giuliani
I mean he did great things
but ya know EVERYBODY did great things
everybody was *here*.


And I'll never forget the nights too,
how dark it was down here
ya know at night, cuz you're so used to being in Manhattan
it's—hey,
I live out on Suffolk County, it gets dark by my house but
    it's still lit
ya know
the first night when it got dark here
I was like wow!
Cuz all you had was spotlights in the front of the building and
    spotlights to the actual ground zero ya know what I mean

and ah . . .

I remember takin' a walk

down to the park and they had the helicopters landin' there
and I went a little further

and it was dark, so dark

and I remember layin' on the grass going

It's unbelievable to think that it was Manhattan that you're
layin' in

ya know it's crazy, crazy

and people come up and go "you alright?"

You go "yeah I'm alright, I'm just chillin'"

ya know

"I need to get my head together."

Everybody understood.


I remember seeing a fire truck being pulled out, a hook and
ladder

and I remember thinking about my dad

ya know

he took me on—

I remember seeing that and makin' me cry ya know

thinking those guys ran down there

ya know

and ya knew someone was with that truck

because you never left the truck alone

wherever they went, there was always someone standing
   next to that truck.

And the truck was just squashed.

I remember being a kid ringing the bell

my father brought me to the firehouse ya know

my uncle was a fireman ya know

we went down to his firehouse.

Ya know I could have been a fireman

when I was growing up I took the test and passed it
   and I just . . .

My father was a fireman.

I just didn't have it in me.

When I walked down to ground zero and

I saw that and said this isn't where I'm supposed to be

I'm better off back here.


And the nights here too were really tough

cuz the guys were here tryin' to sleep

and they—in the middle of the night

a lot of them slept

a lot of them screamed

ya know

you never thought you'd hold a guy like that in your arms

ya know, as he's screaming

but you knew what they went through you know

they were telling ya

and you saw the body parts lined up

it had to be the third day when my wife said, "They found
    forty bodies."

And I'm like ya know

honey I went down there and there's hundreds of body bags
    layin' there

ya know and you're sayin' there's only forty bodies

ya know.


People's eyes were filled with dirt.

They had to wash 'em out.

People couldn't breathe from the dust.

Now we look back

and oh my god what did we run into, ya know.

I'm still sittin' here wondering what the hell I'm breathin'
    here for the last three months

ya know

I remember the chancellor comin' here

and I'll never forget the look on his face

when he says, "I'm gonna be here, I'm gonna show you
    how safe the air is,"

then two days later he was gone.
And I'm like who's he showin' how safe it is,
he didn't show me and ah . . .
my doctor says maybe I should get out of here
and I'm like, well
where am I gonna go
where am I gonna work
you know I got kids
and I move on and hope for the best.

Tim Drinan as Tony Qian

# WHAT MATTERS

Tony Qian, sophomore

*Tony is fifteen years old. He sits at a table in the library,
wearing a white sweater, black pants, and black shoes. He
speaks quietly and with a slight accent—he replaces most
"th" sounds with soft "dh" sounds ("think" becomes "dhink,"
"the" becomes "dhe"). He keeps his hands clasped in his lap
except for a few moments: talking about the human mind,
he motions to his temples, and when he mentions having
grace "inside yourself," he motions to his chest. At the end of
the monologue he stands up and puts his backpack on as he
is speaking.*

I guess . . .
I was sort of in denial the entire day.
I was completely—I just couldn't accept that—
I dunno.

I guess the human mind doesn't have . . .
a tendency to, to think about the more practical things.
More about the things at hand except, uh—

instead of the things that's happening in another country,
    for example.
I guess—I guess I'm still in denial
of what's happened.
Cuz the Stuyvesant environment *[chuckling]* really offers you
    a very good, I dunno, path to . . .
just forget about all these stuff. So much work to do,
teachers giving out tests, all these things that just take up all
    this space
in your head.


*[pause, speaking slowly]*
Grace—being calm, being rational, in . . .
the face of catastrophe, chaos . . .
is something . . .
that not a lot of people can do, but . . . perhaps, um,
think we can do.
Something that's so hard to obtain that people don't realize
how hard it is to actually have it—
um, have it in yourself. Almost, perhaps, unattainable.
Um . . . yeah. That's what I think it is.
Grace is an ideal that, that you could argue, is unattainable.
But that *strive* to achieve it is something that's very
    courageous, on

whoever's part

that wants to try to, to go down—to go down that path to
    achieve

grace,

but I really think it's something that's, um, that's humanly

a very improbable thing to achieve.


I don't think about . . .

this kind of stuff while I'm sleeping—

well, sometimes, well,

sometimes maybe at night before I fall asleep I may just
    have these images in

my head,

of, uh . . .

towers falling down, or something

and donating blood.

People in my neighborhood donating blood.

That was really, really brave, but . . . um . . .

I wish I could have done something like that.


I haven't really thought about it ever since.

I try not to think about it, I guess.

There's nothing I can do about it, so, why think about it.

Yeah, like I said, I guess,

something like this really brings out, uh,

something that you never realized before . . .

you know, maybe, like what we read in Mr. Grossman's
    class, um, about . . .

Oedipus, how he was in complete denial throughout the—

throughout the story.

How stupid he was, how foolish he was, that . . .

he couldn't realize what had—what his true identity was,
    until the very

end.

How it was so apparent, um, that kind of thing really,
    I really,

actually, underst—I kind of—I could actually understand,

why he would be in such a deep denial.


You deny something that . . . that . . .

if you accept it, it will hurt you, I guess, you deny
    something . . .

and your denial could be irrational, but, I guess,

the human mind isn't really, at least, totally filled with
    rationality.

There's a part of the human mind that

just, sometimes, uh, discards rationality, to protect itself, from something . . .

so, I see denial as a form of protection,

from some sort of forces that, if you accept it, it will hurt
you.


It may be painful to some people, I guess it's still good
though.

It's good to bring out.


I don't think I could really say much more about this topic,
so . . . whatever.

*[pause]*

I mean, people debate about it on television,

talk about it, talk about terrorists.

But I mean, what does that, what does that have to do
with me?

I mean, I'm a student. I'm not going out there to fight the
Taliban.

So, yeah, um . . .


But, I dunno, it's our tendency, I guess,

to just, to go back to normalcy and I dunno . . .

I would say forget it, but I don't think that's such a good
word—just

"forget about it"—

to not think about it, I guess, is a better word. You—
you're never going to forget about it but it's so much
easier on you, to just not think about it.


The moment right before a test, that test is the world to you.
Your life depends on it.
And trust me, I feel that way too, but,
after you take the test, you just wonder "so what?"
So what if you get a bad grade?
Or you get a good grade.
What matters . . .
Yeah.

Carlos Williams as Alejandro Torres Hernandez

# WE RUN DIS SCHOOL

## Alejandro Torres Hernandez, senior

*Alejandro is seventeen years old, thin and muscled, with the
movements and rhythm of a Latin dancer. He sits straddling
a chair turned backward, his arms resting on its back, often
gesturing with his hands. He is certain of himself, easy, amused.
He wears a tight black tank top, loose black pants, and
sneakers.*

My week was going great up to that point.
No school,
no homework,
and then I heard about it at home on the internet.
We were going to Tech.

It sucked at first
but then I was actually aiight with going to Tech because
   I didn't want to go to that school on 60th Street.
What was it?
King?
Yeah, King.

~

I wanted to go to Brooklyn Tech because I know
mad people there.
But that other school was a ghetto-ass school.
That first day was cool.
I got to see all my old friends.
That assembly was boring, though—
I fell asleep.


The first day of classes was so boring
but they were mad short
which was cool.
To get through that building
I needed a compass
and climbing those steps
I lost mad weight
which made me mad pissed.
The workload there was no different.
We did what was required.
The schedule was cool, too,
I mean, twenty-six-minute periods.
And every day after school
me and my friends had a fiesta at my boy's house.

~

After that
I got home about eight o'clock.
Homework was no different anyway.
Those weeks dragged on
I was mad happy anticipating our return.
I couldn't wait—
I love my building.

At that final assembly
It was cool
but I fell asleep again.

Back to Stuy finally
cuz we is much better
I mean
we got escalators,
our rooms is better,
me and my boys roam the halls.
We run dis school.
I mean,
I got dis school on lock.
I still like some people at Tech
but I love Stuy!!!

Catherine Choy as Jennifer Suri

# AMAZINGLY RESILIENT

Jennifer Suri,
Assistant Principal, Social Studies

*Ms. Suri is a middle-aged woman with vibrant energy and a
direct gaze. She is thin, with long red hair which she pulls back
with a barrette, and has an open, beaming smile. She wears a
blouse, a long flowing skirt, and heels you can hear clicking
quickly down the hallway from several rooms away. She walks
with purpose. As she speaks, she alternates between moments
of speed and almost manic energy and moments of thoughtful
observation, during which she gazes into space. She begins
thoughtfully.*

Hmmmmm . . . I guess
I'm still walking every morning or after school
and on the way to school
and the way home from school
I always make a point in looking over at
the site at ground zero,
and
just, um

*thinking* about that there—
That there are hundreds of people that . . .
who lost their lives and *still*, their bodies are still there,
it's sorta
almost out of respect
I think about them every time I pass by.
So every day I think about it.


I am glad to be back here
because it's our school.
We feel that . . . umm . . .
sense of *community*
a sense of getting back to normal and I think we, you know,
that it is in terms of being healthy
*physically.*
I think, I think—
the people are saying the air quality is fine now—
I think it is!
The problem
is that
that it can become worse than it is.
Our *imaginations* are far scarier than actual reality.


Well, I'll tell you about one incident

not long after . . .

ummmm . . .

*[long pause]* I think it was while we were still at Brooklyn
  Tech.

And I was on one of those new

*superduper number 6 trains* you know

and umm . . .

there was something *wrong* with the

*announcement* system, you know

so we could hear everything the conductor was saying

and the conductor was CLEARLY *speeding*

I mean this train— *[a little annoyed and scared]*

Have you been on a subway train when it was speeding?

YOU KNOW THAT THIS GUY IS GOING MUCH
  FASTER THAN HE

(or she) IS SUPPOSED TO BE GOING!

This train

was

*rrrripping* from—

it was a number 6 train but it was going express—

and it it it was going

I mean the train was rattling

and you could hear *all* their conversa—

they were talking

and so I thought

*This is so—*

I thought

*huh*

I thought for a moment

WHAT you know

it just *flashed* into my mind

that someone could hijack

a subway train and crash it into another subway train!

Have you ever seen this movie called *The Taking of*

  *Pelham 1-2-3*?

Huh.

I remember watching this movie, this 1970s movie

umm some group

that I don't remember their name

or if they were kidnapping the train for money

  or something

I can't remember stuff

you know

and they kidnap

they kidnap one train on the green line

the 4, 5, 6.

Yeah,

so it flashed into my mind for a second

as the train was *rrrracing* you know

out of control

going *so fast*

and we're hearing all this weird conversation

that we shouldn't be

hearing

that there was something *wrong* . . .

that, that it was . . .

but then I thought, you know

my thought was just

from my *clearly*, uh, vivid imagination. *[laughs a bit]*

But then it stopped and I could've gotten off

   and taken the local

but I stayed on the train and you know—

but we're just coping and adjusting

and you know adolescents are

umm . . .

*amazingly resilient.*

So are the teachers as well.


Teachers with windows . . .

like my window

faces the World Trade Center, so some teachers were

   coming in on the late schedule

so they actually *saw* the plane hit the building.
It may take some of the teachers or students who were
    on the late schedule
longer than others to adjust.
Overall
I think people are doing pretty well
*I'm* doing well . . .


I'm so impressed with
*all* the teachers . . .
*all* the students
*all* the administrators
how we made this transition and just
*picked* things up and
helped each other out
and
have new classes, new buildings, new schedule,
new time zone, and everybody has
a new office and
everybody who worked did the best they could and didn't
complain and umm . . .
we all have things in perspective I think
It's, it's—

it was interesting cuz for the first time almost all the classes

in social studies were sorta
grouped together in the same area
and we had this one big office and they were all working
   and so it
almost brought us all closer together in some ways I think . . .
and in the morning
for the administrators—
oh, it was interesting.
In the morning
we're all in this one office
on the first floor and we—normally in the morning
we're scattered on the tenth floor and
now we were brought together in one office
and it was umm . . .
reassuring
to talk to
and to see everyone
and it was—
it was
kinda nice, actually,
in the morning
*morning* being
huh, ten-thirty.
*[Pause]*

~

I was concerned about it.
I was concerned that . . .
that our . . .
I was concerned for
our student population
the Muslim students we have at school
and not only the Muslim students
but students that people associate with
umm, in any way
with—
the events
for example
some people think that Sikhs
who wear traditional turbans or South Asians—
or if you look South Asian
or you look in any way
Middle Eastern
are targeted
whether you know them or not
so just
in *general*
this kind of
targeting,

discrimination

based on people who were afraid of the

quote "Middle Eastern–looking" . . .

it concerned me greatly.

And, you know . . .

so that . . . it got me really worried.

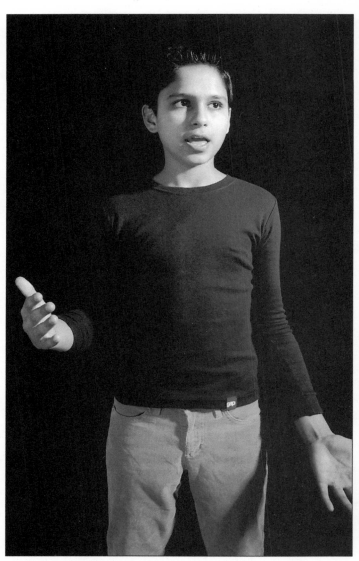

Taresh Batra as Mohammad Haque

# FEARING FOR YOUR SAFETY

## Mohammad Haque, senior

*Mohammad is eighteen years old. He speaks thoughtfully,*
*clearly, expressing deeply felt opinions. He gestures with his*
*hands flat, fingers closed, in straight lines. He wears a tight*
*long-sleeved shirt, tight jeans, boots, and several silver rings*
*on the fingers of each hand.*

That was—
that was probably one of the toughest parts
about September 11th—the backlash.
The trauma or whatever
of actually seeing it
and experiencing it
is something everyone
can relate to
but something everyone can't relate to
is
fearing.
Fearing
for your safety. Personally

not by terrorists either
by us by the general American community.
Fearing for your safety
or more for the safety
of my mother
who covers
her hair
or of my sister or my father
worrying for their safety
from ignorant people
who would do something
to them
because they're Muslim.
And . . .
that's what I was afraid of
like,
the moments afterwards.
Because
I was afraid as everyone else was
about another attack and the safety of the nation
but I was personally worried
about the safety of—
of my family members
because of the backlash against Muslim Americans

and the fact that someone
who doesn't know what they're doing
or someone who is
extremely angry
decides to take their anger out
on a member of my family.
*[very slight pause]*
Or me for that matter.
But characterizing an entire group
by a small
like, minority
of the group
you could say that for
any group
for instance,
white Americans—
How many white Americans
are
are skinheads or things like that
you know, a very very small minority
therefore
you don't characterize
all
white Americans as

people who are racist and
people who hate
other people's color or hate minorities.
It's the same thing with Muslim Americans
or Muslims in general.
Because there is a small
minority of people
who hate American culture
you can't
um . . .
tag all Muslims with that—
If you do then that's just
pure ignorance
and—
you—I mean,
I don't know what to tell you.
You should go out and
learn about the religion because it's just not true.
Like when you're walking down the street—
people are looking at you
in a wrong way
and I'd ask why they're looking at me
and they'd tell you
either with their eyes or whatever

you know
you understand
that they're like
"Yeah, you guys are terrorists" or something
and you just try not to get angry,
and explain the religion.

You know—
I—
I was, uh—
profiled
while on the subway, by a police officer
like
he was giving me
trouble as to where I was going and
what I was doing,
and I just
put out my Stuy ID on him
and I'm like
"I'm going to school.
Is that alright?"
*[grins]*
But it was awesome 'cause
I was never worried about

nothing like that ever happening
while I'm here in Stuy.
Like
I don't know why
but I just have a sense of security while I'm here
and
I know a lot of the people and
if someone were to do something stupid
or ignorant
or of the nature that I was talking about earlier,
then . . .
then
what can we do
I mean
it's only a small amount of people that would do
    something like that
and I guess
they just don't know—
but the general Stuy community
is . . . it's an intelligent community
and everyone knows what's going on, you know

And that's pretty cool.

Liz O'Callahan as Kerneth Levigion

# MISSING WINGS

## Kerneth Levigion (Kern), Building Staff, Theater Manager

*Kern is a middle-aged man with long, prematurely white hair,*
*which he wears in a ponytail. He wears straight-legged jeans, a*
*flannel shirt, black boots, and a walkie-talkie on his belt.*
*Except for rounded shoulders, his posture is good, and he plants*
*his weight on both feet directly under his body. His gestures are*
*deliberate and his arms often move parallel to each other. When*
*he talks about the "corner on the stage" he gestures to an*
*imaginary corner. He looks directly at his audience when he*
*speaks, and pronounces words as if they are falling from his*
*mouth. His words come quickly and he sometimes gets ahead of*
*himself, then pauses to compose his thoughts and continues.*

Okay, the story's . . .
*[sigh]*

I've handled the Stuyvesant American flag more than
    anyone
in this building for the past eight and a half years.

I kept
good care of it
I kept it in this one corner
on the stage
so that nothing would happen to it.
In other words—

When it came here from the old school
one of the wings got broken off the flagpole.
Then during one of the *SING!* rehearsals
the other wing got broken off.
But that's when it went to that one corner.
I cleared out that corner and kept it there.

When we came back
from
Brooklyn Tech
I was looking around the building—
I was in the building a week before everybody else
    trying to get everything
back in order.
Telephones were all messed up.
Televisions—
televisions were irrelevant.

But tryin' to get
the building back into sorts . . .
okay
and one of the things that I noticed
on the stage
was the base
of the flag
and no flag.
So I, I was lookin' all over the building for the flag
   and I couldn't find it.
Just kept
looking
and looking
just
randomly.

One particular morning
I was on the stage
and I saw the base.
By coincidence
somebody showed me one of those—
one of the books
that was published
that had to do with September 11th

and I'm looking through it
looking at the pictures
and I came across a picture
of firemen
installing a flag
on the mast of the World Trade Center
and I looked at the picture and my *jaw* dropped.
It was *our flag*.
She said, "How d'you know?"
I said
I *handled* it more than anybody else
and I
described the flag from one end to the other:
the brown wooden staff
the six-inch brass coupling that held the two pieces together
the gold fringe that went around the flag
the gold tassel dangling
off the top of it
and the eagle missing *both* of its wings.
Now it's
a strange
thing that I said to the
to *The Spectator*
(I dunno if you wanna use this)

but I said:
You know seein' that picture
seein' those wings missing
symbolizes
to me
the Tra—
the fact that the
Trade Center
is gone
okay
the wings symbolize the Twin Towers
they're both gone
but the flag is still waving.

So
since then
after
after seeing the picture
I showed the picture to a couple of other people
including Jimmy Lonardo
who agreed that that was our flag.
I'd wrap the thing up for him so he could take it
over to Avery Fisher for graduation—
it's been at every Stuyvesant graduation for years . . .

So he agreed that that was ours
and
from there
I went to the administration
and I *showed*'em the pictures
and I *asked* them
if we can get in touch with the mayor's office
an' see if we can get our flag back
or at least get some recognition
of the fact
that the picture
in this book
is our flag
on the Trade Center
and they said no.
Said, "We've been in the press *enough*
the last thing we need
is to stir the pot over a flag."

So from there
I basically dropped it
and then
I heard
from

a couple of people
that . . . the flag was taken
it was put on one of the
aircraft carrier
carriers
and sent to Afghanistan
and the flag is now in Afghanistan
That's the last I've heard.

You know that, that flag . . .
you know
people
make comments about that picture
being
equal to
um . . .
drawin' a blank
that one island with a statue . . .

It's Iwo Jima.
I remembered.

# Original Production Notes

*with their eyes* was performed at Stuyvesant High School on February 8 and 9, 2002. The cast and crew were as follows:

*Directors:* Annie Thoms and Ilena C. George
*Producers:* Lindsay Long-Waldor and Michael Vogel

CAST:

Taresh Batra as Katie Berringer and Mohammad Haque
Anna Belc as Katherine Fletcher and Mira Rapp-Hooper
Marcel Briones as Juan Carlos Lopez, Hector Perez, and Haydee Sanabria
Catherine Choy as Ilya Feldsherov, Owen Cornwall, and Jennifer Suri
Tim Drinan as Max Willens, Anonymous man in coffee shop, and Tony Qian
Shanleigh Jalea as Aleiya Gafar, Matt Polazzo, and Jukay Hsu
Liz O'Callahan as Hudson Williams-Eynon and Kerneth Levigion
Chantelle Smith as Anonymous female dining hall worker and Anonymous male custodian
Carlos Williams as Renée Levine and Alejandro Torres Hernandez
Christopher M. Yee as Kevin Zhang and Eddie Kalletta

*Technical Manager:* Ben Spector

*Sound Director:* Ben Softness
*Assistant Sound Director:* John Fu
*Sound Crew:* Daniel Rassi and Elan Schnitzer

*Art Directors:* Elizabeth Behl, Jane Chernomoskaya, and Ryan Muir

*Art Crew:* Carolyn Hayek, Masikl Jackson, Daniella Loh, Liang Shen, Chuck Siegal, Samantha Silverberg, Yinna Wang

*Lighting Director:* Lila Nordstrom

*Assistant Lighting Director:* Giselle Aris

*Lighting Crew:* Amanda Baker, Anna Cummings, Amory Meltzer, Eli Tinkelman, Nina Townsend

*Tech Director:* Matthew Saide

*The Man:* Corey Villiani

*Tech Crew:* John Aliquo, Cale Basaraba, Louisa Bukiet, Caroline Cecot, Anthony Cilento, Emma Coultrap-Bagg, Cynthia Jankowski, Johnathan Juli, Alphonse Lembo, Ann Mary Mather, Val Pechatmikov, Sanjaya Punyasena, Ben Silverman, Laura Stonehill, Phillip Wu

The *with their eyes* set in the Stuyvesant theater.

# Notes on Staging

*with their eyes* was performed with a simple set. In the center of the stage stood a platform with three steps leading up to it on all sides. Two flats flanked the platform, each painted with a gray building fading softly into blue sky. Two columns stood downstage, left and right, each painted with a black skyline fading up into a rainbow-colored sunset. The actors' costumes and props were stored onstage in cabinets behind the two flats, below a trapdoor on the platform, and on hooks behind the columns. The set stood in front of a white scrim. Rear projection was used to display the names of each speaker on the scrim at the beginning of each monologue.

During each act of the play, all ten actors remained onstage at all times. As one actor delivered his or her monologue, the other nine stood, or sat, or took part in silent scenes upstage: during "Golden State," actors passed a long rope of origami cranes from hand to hand; during "Precious Cargo," they sat in rows on the stairs and took out notebooks, as if in a classroom. When actors changed costumes, they did so onstage in full view of the audience, stripping down to a basic layer of black tank top and pants which each wore beneath his or her costume, then visibly taking on another role.

226

"You Need Hope": Both parts were played by one actor, Marcel. The transitions between Hector and Haydee were signified by a minor pause and a change in physical posture.

"Safety Net": The part of the anonymous man who interrupts Max was played by Tim, the same actor who played Max. He began the monologue standing, walking across the stage and pausing to deliver his lines. Behind him, the stairs became a coffee shop, and each of the other nine actors sipped from a paper cup and spoke quietly to each other or mimed reading. After "But that's how she deals with it," Tim moved upstage and took his seat on the stairs—in the coffee shop.

As he shifted into the voice of the anonymous man, he began to change out of Max's clothes and into the man's cardigan sweater, speaking all the while. There were three title projections during this monologue: one identifying Max at the beginning, the second identifying the man as "Anonymous middle-aged man in coffee shop," and the third, after the man identified himself as a Stuyvesant graduate, a correction reading "Anonymous *Stuyvesant graduate* in coffee shop."

End of Act II: Tim slipped offstage in the moment between "Fearing for Your Safety" and "Missing Wings" to take his place at a piano behind the scrim. During "Missing Wings," the cast stood in a line behind Liz. All faced the audience directly as she spoke. After the final words of "Missing Wings," Tim began to play "Windows," a piece he composed shortly after September 11th. He was illuminated with a faint green light behind the scrim. As he played, the other nine actors slowly stripped off the outer layers of their costumes, laying them gently on the stage and walking off as they finished.

*Note:* The photograph Kern refers to in "Missing Wings" is reproduced on page 86 of the book *September 11th: A Record of Tragedy, Heroism, and Hope,* by the New York Magazine Staff. The flag did travel to Afghanistan, and is now back in New York, installed safely in the NYPD Museum.